PEOPLES OF ROMAN BRITAIN

General Editor : Keith Branigan
Professor of Prehistory and Archaeology
University of Sheffield

THE
BRIGANTES

B.R. Hartley

Reader in Roman Provincial Archaeology

University of Leeds

and

R. Leon Fitts

Professor of Classics,

Dickinson College, Carlisle, Pennsylvania

ALAN SUTTON

1988

First published in 1988
by Alan Sutton Publishing Limited
Brunswick Road · Gloucester

ISBN 0 86299 547 7

Typesetting and origination by
Alan Sutton Publishing Limited.
Printed in Great Britain

Contents

For Elizabeth, Mary

and Christopher

Preface

It is inevitable that in writing about the largest *civitas* of Roman Britain we have had to be highly selective, and we are aware that we have tended to concentrate attention on the eastern section of the tribe. But the truth of the matter is that on the one hand the best evidence of change during the Roman period is to be found there, and on the other the splitting off of the Carvetii of the Eden valley (and the Lake District) as a separate *civitas* in the later Roman period has inhibited us from considering that area except in very general terms after the second century. The usual problems of defining the tribal area obtrude, especially for the southern boundary, but we trust that our subjective assessment will serve.

We are lucky in knowing something of the leading personalities among the Brigantes in the first century, unlucky in the loss of the accounts in Tacitus's works both of the first Roman contact with the tribe in the 40s of the first century and their eventual conquest in the 70s. For the later Roman period inscriptions often usefully add flesh to the dry bones of the archaeological evidence, but they can never compensate for the lack of contemporary quantitative information which makes analysis of the economy so difficult.

In the processes of collecting and discussing evidence we have both contributed to all the chapters, though the nominal division is that the first writer was responsible for Chapters 2, 4 and 6, the second writer for the rest.

Over the years we have frequently been stimulated by discussion of many aspects of the Brigantes with friends and colleagues, not least Sheppard Frere and the late, and much-missed, John Gillam. Some other friends have helped us greatly on specific matters, especially Margaret Derrick, Kay Hartley, Andrew (Bone) Jones, David Neal, Patrick Ottaway and Tony Pacitto. Elizabeth Hartley has assisted us enormously both with material in the Yorkshire Museum, York and in the selection of illustrations. For help with the typescript we owe particular thanks to Barbara MacDonald, Carole Fitches and Valerie Wainhouse. Above all we are very grateful to Malcolm Stroud for his drawings, and to Brenda Dickinson for checking the proofs.

That the second writer was able to do research for the book in England is due to generous grants by the American Philological Society of Philadelphia and by Dickinson College, Carlisle, Pennsylvania.
Brian Hartley
Leon' Fitts, 1987

List of Illustrations

Line drawings by Malcolm Stroud

1

Tribal Territory and the Pre-Roman Iron Age

All the non-archaeological evidence for the Brigantes comes from the writings of the Roman period after the invasion of Britain in A.D.43. It is usual to assume that the Brigantes were a confederation of smaller tribes which had been welded into a larger unit during the later stages of the pre-Roman Iron Age. When we first meet them in the Roman sources they are already under the control of a single ruler, namely Cartimandua, the Queen Regnant. However, it should be remarked that classical writers seem sometimes to have used 'Brigantes' to label barbarians in northern Britain in general without greater precision.[1]

The name Brigantes, singular Brigans, is Celtic and is derived from a root meaning something like 'The High Ones' or 'the Hill Dwellers'.[2] Presumably it originally applied only to one tribe which became dominant and transferred its name to the confederation as a whole. This tribe, or at least its leaders, may have been related to the people who settled in the area of Bregenz in Western Austria, and perhaps there was a closer link with the tribe of the same name in Ireland.[3]

That a multiplicity of smaller tribes once existed is suggested by the names for sections of the Brigantes, such as the Setantii of the Fylde,[4] the Carvetii of the Eden Valley, who later became a separate *civitas*,[5] possibly the Gabrantovices of East Yorkshire,[6] the Tectoverdi or Textoverdi[7] and Lopocares of Northumberland,[8] and the conjectured Latenses of the Leeds area (Fig. 1).[9] Clearly many other former tribes must have been incorporated. One can

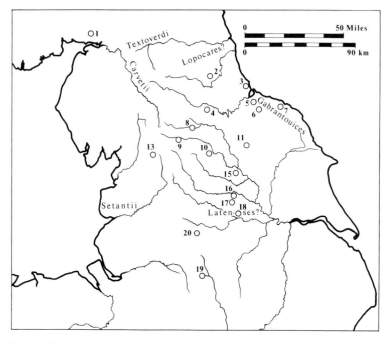

Fig.1.   Iron Age tribes and places mentioned in the text.

Key:
1 Birrens	2 West Brandon	3 Catcote	4 Stanwick
5 Eston Nabb	6 Percy Rigg	7 Roxby	8 Maiden Castle
9 Addleborough	10 Roomer Common	11 Boltby Scar	12 Sutton Bank
13 Ingleborough	14 Ribblehead	15 Grafton	16 Dalton Parlours
17 Barwick-in-Elmet	18 Ledston	19 Mam Tor	20 Almondbury

scarcely avoid the feeling that a remarkable and powerful figure must have been responsible for the amalgamation of the diverse units. Since there is now nothing to suggest that Cartimandua was of Belgic descent, as once was conjectured,[10] it seems likely that it would have been one of her immediate male ancestors who forged the union. This would fit well with the description of her by Tacitus as *pollens nobilitate* – 'powerful in lineage'.[11]

Such a concept of original smaller tribes would be entirely

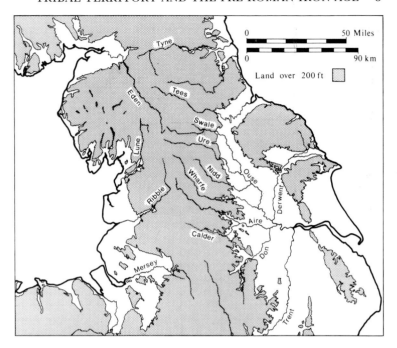

Fig.2.   Physical geography.

consonant with the remarkably varied physical geography of the area (Fig. 2). The major dividing factor was the gritstone and limestone chain of the Pennines. But no simple division into western and eastern groups is possible. The Pennines themselves are divided by the numerous dales traversing them, some like Airedale or Wensleydale offering relatively easy east–west routes, and many of them comparatively heavily populated in the later Iron Age. To the west of the Pennines the Lancashire plain must surely have been one unit distinct from the massif of the Lake District, while the Eden valley offers another natural unit (perhaps extending into Dumfriesshire) which was the home of the Stag People (the Carvetii). East of the Pennines, the Magnesian Lime-stone outcrop, bounded on the east by the marshy flats of the lower Trent and the Vale of York, was densely populated and again is likely to have had more than one sub-unit. The southern part of East Yorkshire, primarily the area of the chalk Wolds, was in the the land of the Parisi. It is not entirely clear where their northern boundary lay, but the northern fringe of the Vale of Pickering, which divides the Wolds from the totally different country of the North Yorkshire Moors, perhaps marks the likely extent. Mr H.G. Ramm suggests that Cawthorn may mark the boundary,[12] but the Vale seems a more likely divide, and the evidence of the square-ditched barrows is not entirely conclusive. We here opt for assigning the Tabular Hills and the Hambletons to the Brigantes. Certainly the bleak peaty moorlands and their associated dales are a total contrast to the gentler Wolds, and to the Tabular Hills north of Pickering, where we must place the Gabrantovices, if they were indeed a sept of the Brigantes rather than the Parisi.[13] The latter's western limit, judging by the distribution of their characteristic square-ditched barrows, must have been the Derwent or the Ouse, more probably the former, as York itself was Brigantian.[14] Further north, the relatively flat country of Durham and Northumberland up to the Tyne Valley cannot easily be subdivided.

Of the rivers in the Brigantian area and its fringes only the Ouse, the Mersey and the Tyne can be regarded as permanently useful for navigation. Most of the rivers issuing from the Pennines are too rocky and uncertain in flow to have been in regular use except in their lowest reaches.

Extent of the Tribal territory

As has been noted above, the evidence for the extent of Brigantia is almost entirely literary and epigraphic, and Roman in date.[15] The second-century geographer Ptolemy notes that their lands stretched from sea to sea and lists various settlements in their *civitas*. These include York, Aldborough, Catterick, Binchester, Ilkley, Rigodunum (often equated with the hill-fort on Ingleborough but perhaps the Roman Fort at Castleshaw),[16] Camulodunum (generally taken to be the native name for the Almondbury hill-fort transferred in the Roman period to the auxiliary fort at Slack) and two places otherwise unknown, Epiacum, thought by some to be Whitley Castle in Northumberland, and Calacum, conceivably Burrow-in-Lonsdale.[17] If dedications to the tutelary goddess Brigantia are admissable as evidence for the extent of the *civitas*, then we may add Birrens in Dumfriesshire (Fig. 1, 1), Castlesteads and Corbridge in the area of Hadrian's Wall, and South Shields at the mouth of the Tyne.[18] Of these, Birrens is particularly significant as showing that Brigantia extended beyond the frontier later defined by Hadrian's Wall. A further group of dedications in West Yorkshire confirms that the Leeds area (Adel) and the upper Calder Valley were included.[19] Since the boundary with the Parisi is reasonably certain, as noted above (p. 4), the only remaining problem is that of the position of the southern limit of the *civitas*. A clue may be offered by the events of A.D. 52–7 in the north, since it seems highly likely that the first forts at Little Chester, Chesterfield and Templeborough, and probably also the vexillation fortresses at Osmanthorpe and at Rossington Bridge, some four miles south of Doncaster, represent Didius Gallus's reaction to the first outbreak of trouble between Cartimandua and her consort Venutius (see p. 16). These would then mark the Don as the likely southern boundary on the east side of the country. That still leaves unresolved the question of the boundary across the Pennines. It is quite uncertain whether the Derbyshire Peak District belonged to the *civitas* of the Brigantes or not. It was, like the northern Pennines, controlled by auxiliary forts for much of the Roman period, however, and if only for that reason we propose to include it here, though with reservations. Little Chester, near Derby, would mark the maximum possible extent of the tribe.[20] On the west side of the Pennines, since Chester fell to the Cornovii on Ptolemy's evidence, the likely southern boundary would be the Mersey estuary and a line from the region of Wilderspool (Warrington), swinging south to skirt the Cheshire plain and aiming roughly for Little Chester seems the most probable one to accept provisionally, especially in view of the events of A.D. 48–9 (see p. 16).

It will therefore be seen that although there are considerable doubts, especially at the southern end of the tribal area, and perhaps also for the Lake District, the *civitas* in the Roman period stretched from the Don to the vicinity of Hadrian's Wall and from the east to west coasts. Since the neighbouring tribes to the south must have had their boundaries fixed by treaty with Rome before A.D.80, this is likely to mean that the pre-Roman extent of the confederation was perpetuated in the Roman system.

The Pre-Roman Archaeology

There is general agreement, though little solid evidence, that the Iron Age population of the Brigantian area was basically descended from the Bronze Age one with greater or lesser influences from incomers belonging to the Hallstatt and possibly also the La Tène traditions. Such evidence as there is for their characteristic artifacts, is limited and thinly spread over the whole of the tribal area, suggesting a sporadic rather than a continuous influx. No doubt this is largely a result of trade, although the physical presence of Hallstatt incomers from the settlements of East Yorkshire may be attested at Grafton and Roomer Common.[21] Nor should we forget the growing evidence for dense settlements on the Magnesian Limestone by people living and farming in a manner akin to some groups in southern Britain (p. 8). Nevertheless, some Bronze Age peoples may indeed have continued for long with their old traditions little changed. Over much of the region Bronze Age finds are both numerically better represented and denser in distribution than Iron Age ones.[22] The ubiquitous barrows of the Bronze Age tell the same tale. One difficulty, however, in distinguishing Iron Age groups until shortly before the Roman conquest is the lack of truly distinctive Brigantian pottery and the rarity of their metal work.

One of the predominant hallmarks of the Iron Age, the hill-fort (in Piggott's terms 'the most typical field monument of the Celtic world'),[23] never became common in our area. The contrast with the extreme south of Britain and the Marches of Wales is notable.[24] Such forts as there are, are small by southern standards, though at least some had defences equally complicated and their sitings are just as varied. If the carbon-14 dates are to be accepted, then it becomes clear that the forts appeared in the north at least as early as the south. Indeed, it has recently been argued that the start of such sites as Mam Tor and Almondbury should formally be assigned to the Bronze Age.[25] Most of the known forts are in the Pennine chain or Cumbria, and one of obvious importance in this group is the massive fort at Ingleborough in Craven. Here, within some 6 ha (15 acres) apparently enclosed by a stone wall, are 19 hut circles.[26] The hill-fort is usually equated with Rigodunum and, if that is correct, it must have been a centre of a princeling before the creation of the confederacy. Some important sites, however, appear elsewhere, notably at Eston Nab just south of the Tees and at Boltby Scar near Thirsk.[27] The major promontory fort at Sutton Bank, enclosing some 20 ha (50 acres), is also taken to be Brigantian rather than Parisian.[28] However, nothing in the records for most forts suggests occupation down to the Roman period, and it is becoming increasingly evident that the habitual use of hill-forts was a phenomenon of the earlier Iron Age in our area. Indeed, the only fortified site which was certainly in use in the first century is Stanwick, which was occupied immediately before the Roman conquest of the Brigantes (p. 8). Whether the conjectured fort at Barwick-in-Elmet was occupied so late as this is totally unknown.[29] Nevertheless, the presence of hill-forts during the Iron Age points to a degree of tribal organization which could scarcely have disappeared subsequently. How permanently or densely the sites were occupied is a matter of conjecture. The abandonment of the hill-forts in general surely suggests that internal feuding and external pressures were not serious enough for major defences to be needed in the late Iron Age.

Since the Wheeler excavation at Stanwick in 1951–2, his interpretation of the site as beginning with a 7 ha (17-acre) fort ('The Tofts'), later enlarged in two phases, eventually to enclose some 300 ha (750 acres), has until recently been widely accepted.[30] Recent work has shown, however, that this interpretation is at least dubious in part and at worst totally wrong. Occupation of a considerable area from the

40s of the first century, if not earlier, is now seen to be more probable, but the precise relationship of the occupation to the defences is still unclear, and it now seems unlikely that three distinct phases of earthworks are involved. However, what is certain is that Roman tableware was reaching the site from the 40s and that Roman roofing tiles were also present in considerable quantity.[31] The latter obviously imply either the existence of Romanized buildings, or the intention to provide some. Such building would certainly have required assistance from people used to construction in the Roman manner, and presumably in this part of the country at that time army personnel would have been called in. The implication is clear: an intention had been formed to build on behalf of a member of the Brigantian hierarchy.

Few of the lesser Iron Age settlements have been investigated by excavation. Where details are known, the general impression is that no appreciable number of houses existed contemporaneously at any. Sometimes it is a matter of a single hut, totally unenclosed or enclosed by a palisade or a bank and ditch, as at West Brandon, County Durham, in its successive stages.[32] More rarely our evidence points to small, compact groups of huts, amounting at most to a hamlet, as at Percy Rigg south of Guisborough.[33] Many areas give the impression of series of adjacent sites, each presumably with a hut or huts, continuing over several miles, as on the Magnesian Limestone on the western fringes of the Vale of York. The likely complexity of such sites is hinted at by the recent work at Roxby, Ledston (Fig. 3) and Dalton Parlours near Boston Spa.[34] The latter has produced about eight round huts set in ditched enclosures covering at least 1.4 ha (3.5 acres).[35] Similar strips of sites obviously existed, normally in unenclosed form, in the Dales. The well-known Wharfedale groups have been plotted by Dr Raistrick[36] and comparable sites exist in Wensleydale, especially on the flanks of Addleborough, and in Swaledale. Recent work in the northern fringes of Cumbria has added many more sites yet to be published in detail.

Therefore, nothing in the record now seems to deny the existence of permanent settlements within our area. The semi-nomadic Brigantians envisaged by Piggott and

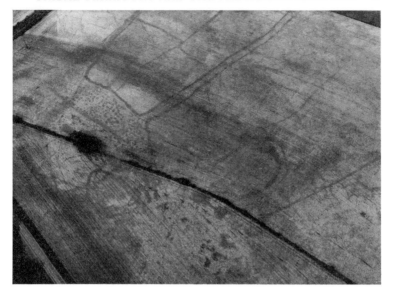

Fig.3. Iron Age occupation at Ledston.

Wheeler look remarkably shadowy.[37] Nor can their proposals, based simply on the evidence of Stanwick, that the Brigantes were only pastoral folk, any longer be accepted. The function of the Stanwick earthworks is certainly not clear, even if its vast defended area might suggest a concern for stock, and the negative evidence of the lack of grain storage pits (an argument from silence as Piggott admits)[38] rests on the investigation of too limited an area belonging to a much larger one. Indeed, there is growing evidence against Piggott's and Wheeler's contentions. A remarkably dense complex of sub-rectangular pits at Ledston implies that grain storage in the manner of southern Iron Age groups was used. The abundant field systems in parts of our area are mostly of doubtful date, though on the evidence of Ledston, Dalton Parlours and Percy Rigg it now seems likely that a higher proportion of them than would once have been believed go back to the pre-Roman stage. Those in Wharfedale, still little known in detail, may for the most part be Romano-British, but some are surely likely to have been in use in the Iron Age, and the nearby settlement at

Ribblehead with its hut circles and enclosures, certainly belong to an Iron Age context.[39] Beehive querns are amply attested and densely distributed in the Pennine dales and on their eastern edge, as well as in the North Yorkshire Moors.[40] Curiously enough, the only part of our region in which they are almost entirely absent is Lancashire. These querns may corroborate the use of arable land in such regions and, though many were perhaps current in the Roman period, some certainly reached Percy Rigg, and presumably other places too, within the late Iron Age. Nor should we forget that the predominance of saddle querns on putative Iron Age sites in our region may simply reflect a high degree of conservatism among the Brigantes, as Challis and Harding suggest.[41]

However, it is clear, despite evidence for the growing of crops, that the main basis of the northern farming economy must have been pastoralism. The very siting of so many of the farmsteads at 200 m to 300 m above sea level, often on steep hill slopes, shows that extensive cereal growing was not in question, and the positioning of the farmsteads was clearly determined by the needs for access to the higher upland pastures, as Applebaum has seen.[42] Among the Pennines and North Yorkshire Moors, too, are linear earthworks comparable to those in the Parisian territory. Certainly not all are Iron Age, but a strong case can be made for some. The usual suggestion is that these are ranch boundaries. At Maiden Castle, on the southern slope of Swaledale west of Grinton, a ditched enclosure of rather less than an acre with a stone wall has a stone-walled drove road leading into it from the east. This is comparable in its general nature to the 'banjo' enclosures of the south, and we are inclined to accept its Iron Age date.[43] The precise composition of the herds is a matter for conjecture, but cattle are strongly represented among the bones found at both Stanwick and Catcote, County Durham, though sheep and horses were also present in appreciable numbers.[44] That these refuse accumulations truly reflect Iron Age husbandry may be in doubt, but they at least provide a general representation of the variety of animals available. It is perhaps not altogether impossible that the famous Aldborough bronze bust of a deity was connected with a native cult concerned with fertility and the protection of herds of cattle. The horns, which we believe are complete, and not part of a terret ring, are remarkably bovine (Fig. 4). Perhaps it is from a priest's sceptre or the like.

From every indication, therefore, a balance between pastoralism and agriculture existed. The former cannot everywhere have been as pre-eminent as was once believed. Pastoralism no doubt predominated in the hill country, while in the lowland areas the normal mixed farming typical of the Iron Age was practised.

Even though a pattern of mixed livelihood is archaeologically attested, other facets of the native economy are less in evidence. More important, the issue of tribal wealth is a clouded one. There is nothing to suggest that the tribe, either in part or as a whole, possessed a currency based on metal. The coins from the Calder valley formerly assigned to the Brigantes prove to be Corieltauvian.[45] An iron currency bar discovered at Sewell's Cave, near Settle, is unique to the region and, while it evokes cultural contacts with the south, it tells us little more. Nevertheless, it is

Fig.4. Bronze of a horned god from Aldborough (½).

improbable that some form of currency did not exist, since many aristocratic luxury items, some from without the confines of the tribe, appear. If, as is likely, native wealth rested on valued commodities within the region, then, given the emphasis on pastoralism, livestock seems the potential basis of social wealth among the Brigantes. A surplus of animals, or the concomitant hides and wool could serve as a substitute for cash, but whether there was a system of barter, or an abstract standard of value attached to the commodities is beyond proof, though probability favours the former. The possibility, however, that the Roman authorities accepted cattle as part of tax in kind is suggested by the large military tannery at Catterick and this perhaps substantiates the recognition of a value system of high antiquity.

As suggested above, one consequence of such wealth was indulgence in luxury items. Without doubt, it also made possible the purchase of material necessities such as salt, metals, and the manufactured goods unavailable in the tribal territory.

Details of Brigantian agricultural products and their impact on the tribe are difficult to ascertain. The types of cultivated crops are not known, though one would suspect that barley and spelt, so well attested south of our region, were the common cereals. That cereal production went beyond a subsistence level is to be doubted. The native population probably will have depended heavily on meat as a dietary staple, complemented by dairy products, some vegetables and cereals. The capability of keeping animals well fed throughout the year seems likely, since Higgs and White have demonstrated that wholesale autumn killing of livestock was not a common Iron Age phenomenon.[46] Indeed, evidence from Catcote and Stanwick show that livestock at each was slaughtered after one or two winters, thus implying both selective culling of stock and availability of some winter fodder. It should also be remembered that the pig probably gave some flexibility by providing fresh meat during the hiatus between seasonal slaughterings and it is interesting that the remains of young pigs were found at Catcote.

Apparently the production of pottery was confined to the immediate needs of the individual settlement or household. Its relative absence, and the miserable nature of that which exists, surely stress the unimportance of ceramics. Emphasis no doubt will have been given to vessels made of other materials, such as leather or wood, of which the wooden bowl from Stanwick may serve as a precise example (Fig. 5). Analogies are to be found, particularly in the cultural assemblages from the crannog sites of Ireland where a decided proclivity for wooden vessels over clay ones existed.[47] Although finer wares, such as samian or pompeian red, reached our area from the south well before the northern Roman advance, and tell of a demand for such pottery, from every indication it was one confined to a small clientèle within the tribe. The native tradition of crude, handmade, gritted pots continued well into the Roman period.

Other home industries will have included basketry and weaving of textiles, as the wicker basket from Stanwick and a variety of weaving implements elsewhere suggest. The date at which iron was first worked in our region is unclear. At least by the mature Iron Age smelting and forging were

Fig.5. The wooden bowl from Stanwick, 15 ins in length.

done at West Brandon where two small bowl furnaces were found within the enclosure.[48] At Catcote, a similar furnace is in a context less certainly Iron Age.[49] Nevertheless, their presence evinces home production, perhaps on a part-time basis, of implements needed by the inhabitants. The iron shears from Stanwick may exemplify *inter alia* a typical tool forged by local blacksmiths. The records also reveal metal-working of a different scope. Decorative metalwork, includ-ing horse and cart fittings, and swords of a distinctive character, were produced in our area (Fig. 6). That these indicate the emergence of specialist schools working for aristocratic clients is a current assumption which is perhaps justifiable in view of the complex technology implied by such objects.[50] It is very satisfactory that evidence of bronze working has now been recognized for Stanwick, and it helps to confirm the impression that the site was the nearest northern equivalent to the *oppida* which had earlier developed in southern Britain.[51]

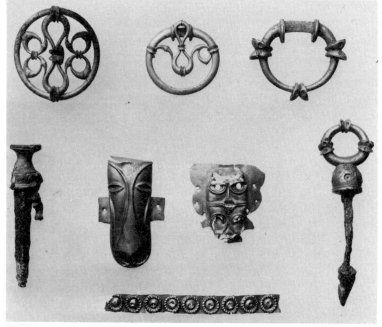

Fig.6.   Part of the Stanwick hoard of metalwork.

2

History: A.D.43–367

The contemporary or near-contemporary sources, all needless to say Graeco-Roman, vary greatly in comprehen-
siveness and value over the range of this chapter. Down to
A.D.85 the literary sources offer a sound basic framework of
military and political history. Thereafter, they are scrappy
and illuminate only brief episodes, such as Severus's campaign or the events of A.D.367. However, the epigraphic
record increases greatly from the early second century
onward, and, with the archaeological evidence, vastly
supplements the written sources, though usually leaving
much open to debate. Since there are several recent general
accounts of northern military history, we here attempt a
change from the normal emphasis on Roman policy or
action to try to reconstruct the events from the Brigantian
point of view. This inevitably leads to a considerable degree
of conjecture, but it is an exercise which seems to us worth
trying.

It must have been soon after the Claudian invasion that
Cartimandua decided to ally herself to Rome, since her
consort Venutius was described by Tacitus in a context of
the mid-50s as 'long faithful to Rome and supported by our
arms.'[1] We cannot know why the queen determined on a
pro-Roman stand, though it may be observed that other
non-Belgic rulers did the same, and the value of Roman
support in any internal or external disputes will have been
apparent to her. It is likely, too, that she will have received
Roman subventions, particularly as the desirability of
having friendly states on the frontier of the Empire was a
standard part of Roman policy at that time. We may be

reasonably certain that she had adopted this course by
A.D.47 at the latest, since the frontier arrangements made
by Claudius's first governor, Aulus Plautius, seems to imply
Brigantian cooperation. Not all the members of the Brigantian confederacy are likely to have backed her whole-
heartedly and it was in the next year that a south-western
section of the tribe rebelled against her authority and
threatened the safety of Ostorius Scapula's expedition to
North Wales.[2] The rebels must have resented being cut off
from their neighbours and perhaps feared loss of trade. The
episode strongly suggests that Cartimandua's centre was
remote from the Huddersfield area, where it used to be
placed by modern scholars.[3]

In A.D.52 the queen's policy was further tried when she
had to decide what to do about Caratacus, the Catuvellaunian exile recently defeated by Ostorius in central Wales.
He perhaps fled to Brigantia thinking to win support from
the rebels of A.D.48. Cartimandua will surely have seen his
presence as a personal threat, quite apart from her obliga-
tion to Rome under her clientship. However, she must also
have known that a move to hand him over to the Romans
would provoke resentment among some elements of the
Brigantes. Perhaps at this stage she was sure of Venutius's
support, as well as of Roman aid if the need arose. But,
within a few years Cartimandua and her consort had
quarrelled, and she needed Roman troops to support her.
When auxiliaries proved insufficient, a legion was also put
into the field.[4] A strong case can be made for assigning the
forts at Strutt's Park near Derby, Chesterfield and Templeborough to the aftermath of these incidents.[5] Perhaps the
vexillation fortresses at Osmanthorpe near Edingley, Not-
tinghamshire and at Rossington Bridge, 6 kms southeast of
Doncaster also belong to the same phase as new postings for
parts of Legio IX, replacing Newton-on-Trent and its third
(unidentified) Claudian vexillation fortress.[6] These sites are
probably poised on the boundaries of the confederation (p. 5
and Fig. 7). The decision to plant them will have been taken
by the governor of the time, Didius Gallus, and although he
may have done so on a request from Cartimandua, it seems
likely that he was anxious to avoid having troops in Brigan-

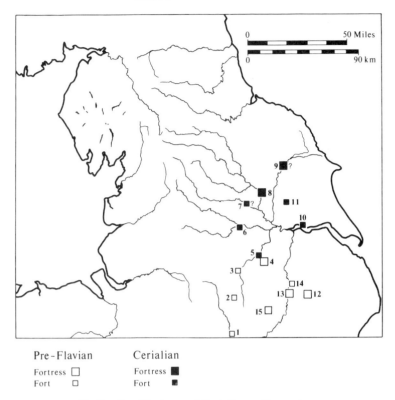

Fig.7.   Pre-Flavian and Cerialian military sites.

Key:
1 Little Chester   2 Chesterfield   3 Templeborough
4 Rossington Bridge   5 Doncaster   6 Castleford
7 Tadcaster   8 York   9 Malton
10 Brough-on-Humber   11 Hayton   12 Lincoln (after A.D.61?)
13 Newton-on-Trent   14 Marton   15 Osmanthorpe

tia itself, where their presence might well have caused considerable trouble. It seems that Cartimandua must have patched up her quarrel with Venutius after this episode, as she was evidently in firm control of the tribe in A.D.61 when it might have been expected otherwise to have joined the Boudiccan rebellion. Nothing more is certainly known of the

relations between the Brigantes and Rome before A.D.69.
The fact that Roman building material is now known from
Stanwick in the pre-Flavian levels has already been
recorded (p. 8). The implication, in view of the almost
inevitable employment of Roman army personnel in the
work, is that building was being done for a member of the
Brigantian royal house. Since the location seems rather far
north for Cartimandua herself, a palace for her consort may
have been involved. Cartimandua's own seat has never been
located certainly. That it lay in the Vale of York seems
almost inevitable. That said, the choice between a site in the
vicinity of York, Aldborough or the suggested one at
Barwick-in-Elmet is impossible on our present evidence
(Fig. 1).[7]

From the late 50s down to A.D.69 Cartimandua evidently
remained dominant. It was presumably late in this period
that the trouble with Venutius eventually came to a head,
Cartimandua divorcing him in favour of his armour-bearer,
Vellocatus. Venutius chose the opportunity offered by the
troubles of A.D.69 to take over the kingdom, having called
in his allies. The struggle for power must have been severe,
and it is a fair inference that Cartimandua's resources
reasonably matched with his, since there must have been
some interval before Roman troops moved, in view of the
current political situation in the Empire and the province.
Furthermore, Venutius required extra forces, possibly some
from outside the confederacy. When Roman troops did
appear, there was a close struggle and, as Tacitus admits,
some reverses for the Roman auxiliary infantry and cavalry,
who alone took the field, because of the discord between the
legions. Cartimandua was rescued and finally disappears
from history, as does Vellocatus. Venutius then controlled
Brigantia and as Tacitus put it, 'Rome was left with a war to
fight.'[8]

It is usually assumed that Venutius then retired to
Stanwick where he stayed until Petillius Cerialis caught up
with him about A.D.72. If he was truly left in control of
Brigantia in A.D.69, however, this makes poor sense. He
would inevitably have had to exercise his control from
Cartimandua's former centre or its neighbourhood. The

implication is that the Vale of York would have been Cerialis's first objective in dealing with Venutius. Furthermore, an approach to it through Parisian territory would make sense, if Venutius's forces controlled the southern approach to the Vale. An attack in this way in A.D.71 would justify Tacitus's description of events in the action against the Brigantes as 'immediate'.[9] However, we cannot entirely rule out an approach from the Doncaster region instead, or in addition. Probability favours the idea that some of the costly battles fought by Roman troops will have been in this sector and that only after initial defeats will Venutius have retreated northwards, where Stanwick is usually seen as the centre of his own section of the tribe.[10] That Cerialis was to some extent consolidating his gains seems certain from the evidence of early Flavian occupation of the forts at Brough-Petuaria, Castleford, Doncaster, Hayton, Malton and the site at York (Fig. 7). The latter, as is well known, blocked the relatively easy crossing of the Vale, thus controlling contact between the Brigantes and the Parisi. Whether Venutius retired on Stanwick, there finally to be defeated, now seems doubtful in view of the recent work.[11] Nor is it known what his final fate was. In view of the undoubtedly pre-Agricolan marching camps across the Stainmore pass, it is by no means impossible that Venutius retired to the Eden Valley or its neighbourhood. What does seem firmly established is that Tacitus was right when he wrote of the greater part of Brigantia being 'embraced in conquest or at least fought over.' No doubt groups of the rebels will have taken to the hills ready to carry on guerilla war against Rome. Is it possible that the tribe of Brigantes placed in Ireland by Ptolemy results from elements of our Brigantes fleeing across the Irish channel at this time (Ptolemy II.2.6)? Soon reports will have reached the hillsmen that the ninth legion was being stationed permanently in their lands, whether at York as a whole, or split between York and Malton, as may seem more likely.[12] Perhaps for a time in A.D.74 the removal of Cerialis from Britain and the concentration on Wales by his successor will have given them hope for a respite. But in the interval they must have had reports of further Roman consolidation in and around the Vale of

York, perhaps even of the dispossession of some native
farms in favour of the legionary *territorium* (p. 69). And soon in
all probability they would have seen renewed activity in the
Pennines, with the appearance of at least one fort at Bowes
on the Stainmore Pass and probably a Roman column
advancing to, and building at, Carlisle.[13] Whether the hills
further south received any attention at this time is doubtful,
though a candidate for a Cerialian or Frontinan date must
be the newly discovered fort at Wensley.[14] The existence of
pre-Agricolan forts at Manchester and Ribchester has also
recently been canvassed.[15] This seems unlikely, however, as
the samian from those sites matches with the material from
the Pennine forts rather than with that from such sites as

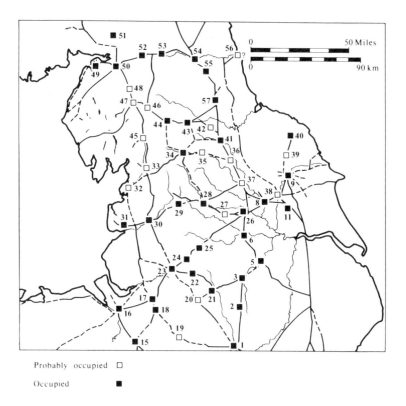

Probably occupied   □

Occupied   ■

Fig.8.   Military sites held under Agricola.

Key for rest of military maps:

1 Little Chester	2 Chesterfield	3 Templeborough
5 Doncaster	6 Castleford	7 Tadcaster
8 York	9 Malton	10 Brough-on-Humber
11 Hayton	15 Whitchurch	16 Chester
17 Northwich	18 Middlewich	19 Chesterton
20 Buxton	21 Brough-on-Noe	22 Melandra
23 Manchester	24 Castleshaw	25 Slack
26 Newton Kyme	27 Adel	28 Ilkley
29 Elslack	30 Ribchester	31 Kirkham
32 Lancaster	33 Burrow-in-Lonsdale	34 Bainbridge
35 Wensley	36 Healam Bridge	37 Aldborough
38 Stamford Bridge	39 Cawthorn	40 Lease Rigg
41 Catterick	42 Carkin Moor	43 Bowes
44 Brough-u.-Stainmore	45 Low Borrow Bridge	46 Kirkby Thore
47 Brougham	48 Old Penrith	49 Kirkbride
50 Carlisle	51 Broomholm	52 Nether Denton
53 Chesterholm	54 Corbridge	55 Ebchester
56 South Shields	57 Binchester	58 Greta Bridge
59 Watercrook	60 Ambleside	61 Hardknott
62 Ravenglass	63 Troutbeck	64 Moresby
65 Papcastle	66 Maryport	67 Caermote
68 Old Carlisle	69 Beckfoot	70 Burgh-by-Sands
71 Stanwix	72 Bowness	73 Birrens
74 Netherby	75 Castlesteads	76 Bewcastle
77 Birdoswald	78 Carvoran	79 Whitley Castle
80 Greatchesters	81 Housesteads	82 Carrawburgh
83 Chesters	84 Halton Chesters	85 Rudchester
86 Benwell	87 Wallsend	88 Newcastle
89 Chester-le-Street	90 Lanchester	91 Risingham

Doncaster, Castleford, Malton, York, or even Carlisle. The same applies to Walton-le-Dale, whatever the nature of the site. At this stage levies of local tribesmen may have been demanded by the army for some of the rough labour of road-construction. And probably from Cerialis's action onward some will have been drafted into the army among the *cohortes Brittonum,* already in existence by the Flavian period.[16] Hope, however, was still there and it was not until the second or third year of Julius Agricola's governorship, A.D.79–81, that the whole of the Brigantian area, Cumbria apart, was finally garrisoned.[17] We may surmise that the

result of Cerialis's action, and of recruiting, was the disappearance of many of the men of fighting age, since
Agricola apparently met with no serious resistance to his
advance. Down to A.D.80, there will have been many
Brigantians who had not seen a Roman soldier. The result
of Agricola's cordoning of the north with forts will have
been that even the remote areas were within reach of patrols
(Figs 8 and 9). The natives would play no part in fort
building, except possibly in the rough work of collecting
materials, but they will inevitably have been required to
provide labour in the building of roads under supervision of
the army, and they may have had to contribute to the
mining activity in the Pennines attested from A.D.81.[18] As
always with armies in the field, there will have been cases of
ill-treatment of the natives. Furthermore the construction of
roads, forts, and their annexes will have involved considerable expropriation of land. We may also suspect that local
inhabitants may have been affected by the *territoria* assigned
to the York legion (p. 20) and to auxiliary units, assuming that
was already done in the first century. In our area the fort at
Chester-le-Street is known to have had a *territorium* in the
third century. In the provinces in general, auxiliary *territoria*
and *pratae* (ranches) are attested.[19] The subsequent appearance of tax collectors on the scene will have done little to
reconcile the natives to their new position, though some will
from the first have chosen to move to the *vici* of the forts,
there to make their living off the army, but also to some
extent to be under army control, in practice if not in legal
theory.[20] Military government of newly-won areas is only to
be expected, and it is of particular interest that a *centurio
regionis* is now known for Carlisle in the period A.D.95–
105.[21] The function of such officers seems to have been one
of policing the region in question and one cannot help
wondering whether there may be a connexion with western
Brigantian attitudes to Rome. Could the undefined region
be the presumed *pagus Carvetiorum* later detached from
Brigantia (p. 31)?

By the end of the century, Brigantia seems to have been
pacified and there is no positive evidence that natives of the
area took a hand in the disturbances which seem to have

Fig.9. Bainbridge under snow.

attended the Trajanic withdrawal from Scotland, unless possibly the likely destruction of the Corbridge fort is to be attributed to them rather than, as seems more probable, to Scottish tribesmen.[22] The creation of Trajan's new frontier on the Stanegate, the road joining the Solway and the Tyne,

will probably have had little effect on them. Contact with
the area of Brigantia beyond the frontier in southwest
Scotland will still have been relatively easy, and the widely-
spaced series of forts and fortlets can never have entirely
prevented clandestine movement or casual raiding across
the frontier. Traders carrying goods beyond the frontier will
have been expected to pay custom duties, at five per cent.[23]
Evasion will again have been relatively easy, however.

The Northern Frontier.
Hadrian's biographer, giving a summary of the state of the
Empire at his succession in A.D.117, says laconically that
the Britons 'could not be kept under Roman control.'[24] The
Brigantes were once blamed for this, but recent work on the
Roman forts in the Pennines and their east flank has shown
conclusively that the burnt layers attributed to their insur-
gence are in reality Roman demolition layers.[25] Nor would
Hadrian have largely withdrawn his garrison from those
areas if they had so recently been troubled. It is just possible
that rebellion was centred west of the Pennines, where
Hadrian retained garrisons, but direct evidence has not
been forthcoming and it seems much more likely in view of
the earlier disturbances and the Hadrianic investment in
the frontier, that it was the tribes in southern Scotland who
were causing trouble. If Richmond and Wright's restoration
and interpretation of the Jarrow monument commemorat-
ing the building of the Wall is correct, the barbarians had
been scattered, and this would imply people outside the
province in view of the specific statement elsewhere that the
Wall was built to separate Romans and barbarians.[26]

Hadrian's own visit to Britain, where he 'put many things
to rights,'[27] clearly prompted the decision to build the Wall,
which eventually turned out to be his most complicated
frontier. As there are good, recent accounts of the Wall and
its setting, we need not discuss its details here, but we
should consider its impact on the Brigantes.[28] In the first
place the sheer scale of the project and the orderly, sys-
tematic work applied to it must have been exceedingly
impressive to them. Hadrian no doubt made it clear that
they were now Romans and were expected to behave as

such, especially as they were both symbolically, and to some
extent practically, cut off from their northern neighbours.
The initial scheme indeed gave them many exits to the
north, through the milecastles, but only under strict military supervision. The creation of the military zone defined
by the Vallum to the south of the wall was probably more
disturbing to them. In the first place it must have meant
considerable commandeering of land (something of the
order of 4,800 ha (12,000 acres), quite apart from the land
taken for the military zone of the Cumbrian coastal
defences). The removal of settlements falling within the
zone, like the one at Milking Gap, was also involved. That
many more existed is implied by the frequency with which
plough marks have been noted under forts on the Wall.[29]
Vici associated with the new forts also had to be south of the
Vallum. Secondly, however, it led to an even stricter control
of traffic across the frontier, since this was now directed
either through the forts, or to special crossing points, such
as the Portgate and later the Knag Burn gate near Housesteads. Furthermore, the isolation of those Brigantes
beyond the Wall in the western sector must have seemed
more extreme. The planting of forts in that area at Birrens,
Netherby and Bewcastle presumably had at least two purposes, both defence of the detached part of the province and
also the policing of what was clearly a sensitive area. And
the extension of the Wall system far down the Cumberland
Coast stressed Hadrian's determination to prevent casual
raiding and smuggling as far as possible. We should perhaps emphasise that from the Roman point of view, the
Wall was primarily a base for forward operations to deal
with developing threats before they matured. Hadrian, at
the time of the building of the Wall, removed the remaining
garrisons in east Yorkshire and evidently thinned them very
considerably both east of the Pennines and in the hills
themselves (Fig. 10).[30] This must have pleased the local folk
not a little, but equally it was no doubt coupled with
expectation of a higher degree of romanization in the area.
As we shall see, the emergence of Aldborough as the tribal
administrative centre, is likely to belong to this stage (p. 41).
However pleased these sections of the tribe may have been,

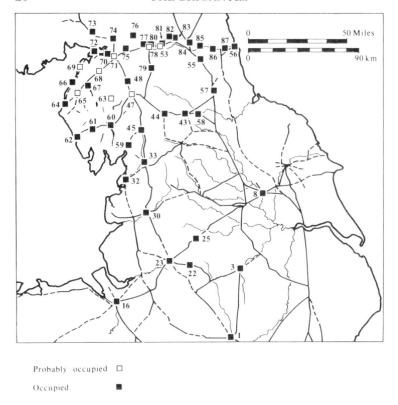

Probably occupied □

Occupied   ■

Fig.10.   Military sites held under Hadrian (see p. 21 for the key).

there was probably less joy west of the Pennines when no
sign of reduction of garrisons came. Indeed Hadrian seems
to have added to them, since the linking of the coastal sites
via Hardknott and Ambleside to the series of forts on the
main road north apparently happened now. Evidently all
the forts from Manchester northwards to the Wall were still
being held, and it is not surprising, therefore, that we see no
sign of the emergence either of towns or of Romanized
farms. The implication of all of this is that the western
tribesmen were of doubtful loyalty. (The idea that garrisons
were retained there simply because there were troops who
had to be quartered somewhere is scarcely convincing. The
contrast with the other Brigantian regions is too extreme.) It

was also in Hadrian's reign that the Brigantes had to get used to a new legion in their midst. Legio IX had been withdrawn from Britain by A.D.120 and was replaced at York by Legio VI Victrix, brought from Vetera in Lower Germany by Hadrian's governor Platorius Nepos in A.D.122, it seems.[31]

The decision taken about A.D.139 to reoccupy Scotland must have affected the Brigantes in several ways. In the first place the military grip on much of their territory was further relaxed: more forts now went, notably Melandra, Slack, Castleford, Doncaster and Lancaster. Secondly, Hadrian's Wall, the Cumbrian coastal system apart, was now systematically (and perhaps symbolically) put out of commission. The breaching of the mounds of the Vallum and the filling of its ditch with the spoil at close intervals, is well attested.[32] Similarly the milecastle gates were removed, and it is not impossible that holes were made through the wall itself.[33] Few Brigantians will have been sorry to see it go. Despite the shortage of troops for the new Scottish garrisons, it is noteworthy that most of the area west of the Pennines was still firmly policed, a fact which underlines what we have suggested above about local loyalties there.

So much is clear. The next matter requiring discussion is what happened in the north in the 150s. This has been linked by some historians, including one of us, to an enigmatic passage in Pausanias's *Description of Greece* (8.43.3). There are so many doubts about both the date and context of the passage in question that it is best not to rely on it.[34] The remaining evidence is all circumstantial, but it carries some cumulative weight. First, no one doubts that Scotland was for a time abandoned, at least some of the auxiliary forts being demolished by Roman troops rather than enemy action. Coins of A.D.154–5 with a reverse of Britannia dejected gave a hint of military action in the province.[35] Since Hadrian's Wall was being set right in A.D.158 under Julius Verus,[36] the implication is that it had once more become the frontier. Similarly the fort at Birrens, previously burnt, was reconstructed by A.D.157–8.[37] Reinforcements for all three British legions were drafted from the two Germanies under Julius Verus and landed at

Newcastle upon Tyne.[38] Regarrisoning of one of the Pennine forts is specifically dated to Verus's governorship[39] and
many of the others were reoccupied, on the evidence of
pottery, at this general period. The first Antonine fort at
Lancaster was burnt, and there may be some hint of
contemporary destruction at Ambleside.[40]

How can these facts be explained? One possible interpretation is that the Caledonian tribes either defeated the army
seriously, or otherwise made it impossible to hold Scotland.
Consequently Hadrian's Wall was recommissioned as the
frontier, extra legionaries being called in to help with the
work. Regarrisoning of the forts in the hinterland would
then be seen merely as a matter of finding suitable sites for
the rest of the evacuated units. The burning of Lancaster
and Birrens (and perhaps sites in the Lake District) would
presumably have to be explained as accidental or irrelevant.
In any case the Scottish system would certainly not have
been abandoned without a punitive expedition coming
swiftly. Re-establishment of Hadrian's Wall as the frontier,
and the re-imposition of garrisons in the Pennines, and to
some extent on their east flank, must have been widely
resented by many of the Brigantes and seen as a reversal to
past conditions. The alternative explanation, although not
universally accepted, is that the observed facts are best
explained by the assumption that an internal rebellion in
Brigantia led to the need to pull the army back from
Scotland. Despite the circumstantial nature of the evidence,
this explanation seems to account for the facts more satis-
factorily. Since the sites with evidence of destruction at this
time all lie west of the Pennines, it seems likely that the
scene of action was there.

When Scotland was regarrisoned shortly afterwards, army
units in the hinterland, and on Hadrian's Wall, must have
been thinned, but this time there is no evidence of decom-
missioning the Wall itself, and one might suspect that not
all of the hinterland garrisons were removed. In any event,
the renewed occupation of Scotland was short-lived, and it
seems probable that by A.D.163 Hadrian's Wall had once
more become the basic frontier, and that most of the forts
behind it in Brigantia were garrisoned.[41] Changes to Had

rian's Wall at this period probably involved both the addition of the Military Way, the through road close to the Wall, and perhaps also the recommissioning of the Vallum which would have led once more to restriction of free passage to the north (p. 25). Presumably it was now that the remaining turf wall was replaced by masonry, since it would be in a poor state, even if not breached on the evacuation in A.D.140. Reimposition of military control over the hill country and to some extent its eastern flank, where sites like Malton, Catterick and Ebchester were reoccupied, and at least one new fort appeared (at Chester-le-Street), must have evoked resentment (Fig. 11). At one time, when the later second-century burning attested at some sites on, or near, Hadrian's Wall and in forts in the Pennines was

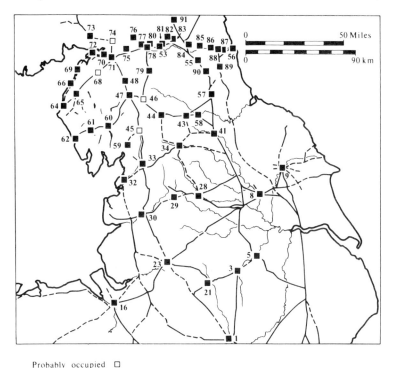

Probably occupied   □

Occupied   ■

Fig.11.   Military sites held c.A.D.165 (see p. 21 for the key).

attributed to A.D.196–7, it was possible to think in terms of eventual Brigantian reactions. In recent years, however, it has become usual to assign the destructions on Hadrian's Wall to the reign of Commodus and to connect them with Cassius Dio's statement that a wall in Britain separating them from Roman garrisons was crossed by an enemy who killed a legate, or governor, and badly mauled the troops under his command.[42] Since the destroyed sites are all in one sector of the Wall, this interpretation seems reasonable. Destruction in A.D.196–7 may seem even more likely, however, as it would be difficult to account for the widespread destructions in hinterland forts otherwise and it still seems more likely to us that they result from revolting Brigantes taking the opportunity to destroy what they could at a time when the governor of Britain had removed many of the British army units to fight for him on the Continent against Septimius Severus's forces in A.D.196–7. There are hints at such sites as Bainbridge and Ilkley that some of the barracks were occupied at the time of the destruction and the implication is that small detachments had been left to look after the forts, but that they proved insufficient to deal with determined attacks by the natives.[43] Severus's first three governors of Britain were all active rebuilding forts in Brigantian territory, and there are some grounds for thinking that Brigantian unrest may have continued down to A.D.206 or so.[44] Shortly after this, Brigantia saw the arrival of the emperor himself, who established his head-quarters at York, and with his elder son, Caracalla, campaigned for two seasons against the Caledonian tribes.[45] Some of the Praetorian Guard will have accompanied Severus to Britain, and their barracks during their stay will presumably have been at York, since Severus probably had a palace there, and an enclosure attached to the fortress is likely to have housed them.[46] York at this period was not only an imperial residence, Severus dying there in February 211, but it also became the capital of the province of Lower Britain created by Severus. Its governor was the legate of Legio VI.

That Severus and his governors were actively rebuilding on Hadrian's Wall is firmly established by a series of

inscriptions on the Wall and at Corbridge.[47] Indeed, some
of his biographers attribute the building of the Wall to
Severus.[48] It seems likely that it was under him that the
Vallum finally disappeared as the southern boundary of the
military zone. Civilian settlement was then allowed close to
the forts. After Severus's death the newly-won territory in
Scotland was soon given up, and neither there, nor in
Brigantia, do we find any compelling evidence of anything
other than routine military activity during the rest of the
third century.[49] Indeed, there is considerable evidence that
the installations on Hadrian's Wall became very ruinous,
and some of the forts may well have been totally abandoned.[50] However, there is so far no comparable evidence
for forts in the hinterland of the Wall, and they seem to have
been fully garrisoned throughout. The *Civitas Carvetiorum*,
with its centre presumably at Carlisle, is first attested as a
separate organization in the Eden valley before A.D.268.[51]
It is usually held that it was a third-century creation, though
this is obviously not certain. It might seem tempting to
relate its appearance to Pius's deprivation of Brigantian
territory related by Pausanias (p. 27), though that is even more
speculative. Whenever the separation happened, it will no
doubt have been a blow to the Brigantian pride.

Constantine's father, usually known as Constantius
Chlorus, seems to have tightened up discipline on the Wall
and rebuilt at least some of the forts, as well as undertaking
further campaigning in Scotland before his death at York in
A.D.306 when Constantine (Fig. 12) was proclaimed
emperor by his troops. Several forts in Brigantia have
produced evidence of rebuilding in the late third or early
fourth century, but there is nothing to show that the work is
all contemporary or assignable to Constantius, though it
has often been suggested that the impressive new front to
the fortress at York is his work.[52] The contemporary
reorganization of military and civil government probably
had little effect on the Brigantes.

As far as the Brigantes south of the Wall are concerned,
there is no evidence that the third century, or indeed the
fourth century down to A.D.367, was anything but a time of
profound peace. And we shall later be discussing the

Fig.12.   The York head of Constantine, from a statue twice life-size.

considerable development of civilian institutions during
this period. The sector of Brigantia north of Hadrian's Wall
was the scene of disturbances in the fourth century and it
seems clear that the outpost forts at Bewcastle, High
Rochester and Risingham were destroyed in A.D.342.[53]
Brigantia does not seem to have been affected by the coastal

raiding which disturbed the south, though the general reorganization of army methods in the early fourth century led to the construction of new forts at Piercebridge, Newton Kyme, and Elslack, which are best interpreted as having to do with the use of highly mobile forces attested for this period.[54]

3

Communications and Urban Settlement

Nothing is known of the pre-Roman routes in Brigantia except what may be inferred from the topography of the terrain and the positioning of such sites as Stanwick, clearly intended to control movement north on the east side of the Pennines, but also movement across the Stainmore gap followed later by a Roman road (Margary 82). With the Roman conquest of the north the picture changed dramatically almost overnight (Fig. 13). Forts planted under the Flavian governors demanded joining roads, and almost without exception the road network in Brigantia can be explained by military needs. Perhaps the somewhat mysterious road (Margary 80), ultimately joining Stamford Bridge and Newcastle upon Tyne, but without any certain sites of Flavian forts, is an exception. It is unlikely, despite I.D. Margary's interpretation, to be anything to do with a campaign route since it avoids such key points as York, Catterick and the Stanwick area.[1] What has to be visualised in the period A.D.71–83 or so is the careful surveying of routes and the construction of the roads themselves, no doubt using native labour under legionary control, and making use of local quarry-pits. The results are impressive in terms of miles constructed alone (1400 kms, 850 miles minimum in the period) but scarcely less so in the detailed selection of routes and bridging skills implied in an area of difficult terrain. Such roads as the Stanegate (Margary 85) or even more markedly that from Ambleside to Ravenglass (Margary 740) provide detailed pictures of the engineering problems overcome.[2] We may well add the famous Blackstone Edge road (Margary 720a) as one of the few

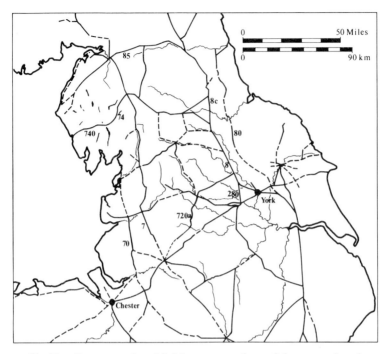

Fig.13.   Roman roads, with Margary numbers of those mentioned.

surviving examples of central ribs, transverse stones attesting gang-building, and the use of a later loop to an earlier gradient for easing travel.[3] If Richmond's interpretation is right, then we also have evidence for the use of the skid-pan brake in the steeper gradients. For examples of bridges, we can turn to such routes as Dere Street in County Durham (Margary 80). Narrow defiles may simply be crossed by timber bridges supported at each edge on an embankment, as at Hunwick Gill.[4] However, crossings of major rivers were frequently needed in our area, and one only has to name such rivers as the Ouse, Nidd, Ure, Swale, Wear, Tyne, Ribble and Lune. Often the positions of the Roman bridges are clear enough, but few traces of them remain. Most impressive are the Tees crossing at Piercebridge, where recent work has revealed an abutment in massive masonry, and the bridges on Hadrian's Wall over the north Tyne at

Chesters and the Irthing at Willowford. Originally designed as narrow bridges simply carrying a walk, the last two were later impressively widened to carry both the Wall and a major road.[5] Normally, such bridges had stone abutments and piers with timber superstructure.

The basic pattern of roads in the North involved what were in effect the predecessors of the A1 and M6 (Margary 8 and 7) as the main lines of communication, with cross-links through the Pennines wherever the topography was suitable. The positioning of the initial forts was obviously determined by the need to control blocks of country effectively (cf. Tacitus, *Agricola* 20), and this was done by planting them in the major dales. The roads thus effectively link the forts to lateral roads, and hence, ultimately the legionary fortresses also, like two adjacent trees rooted at Chester and York with intermingling branches (Fig. 13).

Here and there the network retains hints of the earlier campaigns and organization. For instance, Margary's route 28 comes up through Doncaster and Castleford to swing northeast to York. From York it is continued north to Aldborough. This must surely reflect the arrangements under Cerialis or Frontinus. Later, no doubt in the Agricolan period, in view of the late initial date of the fort at Newton Kyme, a by-pass to York was in effect provided by Margary 280, the Rudgate.[6] Other later additions and alterations to the system of roads will have included the provision of the apparently non-military route Margary 80, noted above, and Margary 70, joining Wilderspool on the south bank of the Mersey to Lancaster, for which direct military considerations were perhaps secondary.[7] But the Lake District also called for attention later. Agricola had avoided it; his successors had to provide routes through the most difficult country, for instance linking Ambleside and Ravenglass via the notoriously difficult Wrynose Pass (Margary 740) or the interesting ridge route of High Street leading from Ambleside to Brougham (Margary 74).[8] Further north eventual provision of a frontier road along Hadrian's Wall was delayed until the Antonine period because the Agricolan Stanegate had been held to be adequate by Hadrian. But in northern Cumbria a complicated series of routes for supplying the coastal forts will have been needed. Similarly, the military needs called for means of rapid signalling in emergency. Notable in the north is the Stainmore system of signal-stations joining York with the senior officer on the Wall at Stanwix.[9]

It should be pointed out that it is from such route-books as the Antonine Itinerary of the early third century that much of our evidence for Roman place names stems. Although only half a dozen names in Brigantia are not attested elsewhere, the Itinerary usually has less corrupt versions than the Ravenna Cosmography and the Notitia Dignitatum. The Itinerary's purpose is less than clear; the suggestion usually made is that it lists posting-stations of the *cursus publicus*, perhaps recording routes of specific journeys made by emperors, officials or troops on the move. However that may be, it will be clear that the posting system will have called for *mansiones* and *mutationes* along all the major routes in the provinces. We should therefore expect them on our trunk roads to the north, as well as on some of the more important cross-links, such as that between Chester and York and on the line of Hadrian's Wall. Structures thought to be *mansiones* occur at Melandra and possibly Slack before the middle of the second century. The former is an elaborate building, including at least thirteen small rooms suitable for use as bedrooms, and conceivably with a second floor, if we may accept the narrow stairwells suggested.[10] For Catterick we must await the full report, but the *mansio* excavated in 1958–9 is thought to be Hadrianic, to have covered an acre or so, including its bathhouse, and to have had elaborate architectural fittings, with provincial versions of Corinthian capitals.[11] No doubt most of the *mansiones* on the trunk routes were as elaborate. In order to complete the system of posting-stations south of Catterick we must postulate others at Aldborough, Castleford and Doncaster, no doubt with some intermediate *mutationes*. North of Catterick inscriptions of *beneficiarii* attached to the governor's staff hint at similar establishments at Binchester (*mansio?*), and Lanchester (*mutatio?*),[12] the system being completed at Corbridge, where a structure on Site II excavated in 1906–7 has been interpreted, no doubt correc-

tly, as a *mansio* with three periods of construction (see p. 62).
On the line of Hadrian's Wall a *mansio* is reasonably certain
for Chesters. There was undoubtedly one at Chesterholm in
the later second century. This well illustrates the simple
kind of building to be expected in the frontier regions.[13] It
was perhaps replaced by a *mansio* at Housesteads where
there was a *beneficiarius* active in the third century.[14] The
other building usually taken as a *mansio* is at Benwell,
alongside the Vallum crossing, but evidently of third-
century date.[15] Perhaps it was a customs post rather than a
mansio.

Finally, it is worth noting that the Brigantian area has
yielded nearly half of the inscriptions on milestones found
in Roman Britain. This is perhaps nothing but the hazard of
survival. Most of them are third- or early fourth-century,
but they should not be taken as indicating special attention
to repairs at that time. Named places are rare on the stones:
only York in the guise of 'Eb' at Castleford and Brough-on-
Noe (Navio) on a stone found at Buxton.[16]

Naturally most of our evidence for the use of inland
waterways comes from the distribution of traded goods, often
from abroad. These will be dealt with later (Chap. V), but
some general points should be made here. First, there is a
clear distinction between the east and west side of the *civitas*.
The Ouse with its tributaries, and the Tees and Tyne, all
offer good communication inland. Between the Mersey and
the Solway-Eden system, only the Lune estuary as far as
Lancaster is likely to have been used at all extensively,
though the existence in that region of Portus Setantiorum
should not be forgotten, since an estuary siting is likely. The
coastal sandbanks are, however, tricky and perhaps the
activity of a unit of bargemen in the area is determined by
the need to tranship supplies to vessels of shallow draught
for consignment to Lancaster and other destinations.[17]

To revert to the east coast, it is evident that the Humber–
Ouse system was in regular use as an inland route, as
several inscriptions and the provision of quays in York
attest. One of the stones must be noted here, since it serves
to remind us that Lincoln was joined to York by an inland
system, involving the Foss Dyke to the Trent. The third-

century merchant M. Aurelius Lunaris was an official of the colleges of *Augustales*, devoted to upholding the Imperial Cult in both the towns. He presumably had business affairs in both and no doubt travelled between them frequently. The extent to which the Ouse system was used above York is a matter of guesswork. Small vessels of the kind better known from the Low Countries would have no difficulty in penetrating much higher up the Aire, Wharfe, Nidd, Ure and Swale than their confluences with the Ouse. Similar arguments may apply to the Tees, and certainly to the Tyne, where significantly bargemen again appear, this time specifically stated to be Tigris *barcarii*.[18]

Towns are usually, and rightly, taken to represent the highest level of civilian development in the Roman provinces. Their definition is by no means easy, but for the Roman world we have essentially to think of nucleated settlements with administrative and, or, marketing functions together with a reasonably high degree of planning and with buildings at both public and private levels in approximation to Roman architectural style. A major problem lies in deciding where to draw the line between the towns and the larger *vici* attached to auxiliary forts. In what follows we propose to treat .only Aldborough, the civil settlement on the south bank of the Ouse at York, Catterick and Corbridge as towns. Compared to southern Britain their density is low, and within the *civitas* there is a striking discrepancy between the east and west sides of the Pennines which must at least in part reflect the relative degree of Romanization, though as we have seen in chapter 2, military considerations also affected the issue. It should here be noted that Carlisle, probably in effect the western equivalent of Corbridge, and Kirkby Thore, perhaps to be equated with Catterick, almost certainly should be ranked as towns in the later Roman period, but they then fell to the *civitas* of the Carvetii.

The Civitas Capital

Curiously enough the only evidence that Aldborough near Boroughbridge was the *civitas* capital of the Brigantes comes

from one of three entries in the Antonine Itinerary, where
the town appears as Isurium, Isuriam and Isubrigantum.[19]
Although only the last entry preserves the tribal name in the
genitive plural, its evidence is conclusive for Aldborough's
status.

Nothing is known of any pre-Roman settlement under the
town, though the vicinity of Aldborough was clearly important in early prehistoric times, as the concentration of henge
monuments in the area shows. The Devil's Arrows, three
large monoliths known to have had at least one more
companion in an arc, are also to be connected with early
prehistoric rites. Whether they played any part in the Iron
Age cults is a matter for conjecture, though there can be no
doubt that the bronze bust of a horned god from Aldborough harks back to a pre-Roman cult (Fig. 4).

The earliest evidence at Aldborough for Roman activity is
from pottery of Flavian date, including some decorated or
stamped samian ware of the 70s rather than later. Normal
spacing of forts north of York would require posts at
Aldborough and Healam Bridge to fill the gap between it
and Catterick. As yet, however, nothing is certain of the fort
at the crossing of the Ure, though a stamped tile of legio IX
suggests military activity before Hadrian's reign. Timber
buildings of Flavian date have significantly been found
under the part of the later town that is closest to the river,
buried under the city wall and northwestern bastion and
apparently deliberately demolished.[20] Usually these are
interpreted as the remains of a *vicus* of the missing fort, but
there is no apparent reason why they should not be internal
buildings of the fort. Excavation in 1961 brought to light a
timber building of the Flavian period, with three periods of
a masonry structure succeeding it, in the vicinity of the east
gate.[21] Although this building has not been published, its
presence greatly expands the known limits of the first-
century settlement, which can now be seen to have spread
over some 7 ha (17 acres). The normal pattern of early
military occupation in our area would lead us to suppose
that the Aldborough fort would be evacuated under Hadrian
(p. 25). It is no difficult matter to imagine that some substantial part of the civilian population would remain behind

when the fort went, a pattern of events which had been normal further south in Britain in the Flavian period. Further civilian development would then be likely to occur, and it is perhaps at this period that the former *vicus* was chosen as the administrative centre for the *civitas*. Certainly there is a marked increase in the quantity of pottery recorded from the Hadrianic period onwards, and such a move would now accord with the policy of Romanization in the hinterland of Hadrian's Wall.

Unfortunately, there is little specific evidence for the building of the town, and only a hint of one public structure may be discovered (Fig. 14). Ecroyd Smith records part of a large building north of the church.[22] It had a double row of stone walls parallel to each other, 5.5 m (18ft) apart and above 70 m (*c.* 229.5 ft) long. These were joined by transverse walls of which Smith marks eight in his plan. The walls were all mortared and 0.9 m (3 ft) thick. The position of this large structure at the centre of town strongly suggests that it is to be identified as the *forum*, in Britain a building combining market, town square, municipal offices, town hall (*basilica*), law courts, official shrine, and the meeting place of the tribal council (*ordo*). Its entrance will presumably have been central and on the axis of the road from the north gate. Such a position for the *forum* may be paralleled at London, Silchester and Gloucester. Smith's walls undoubtedly suggest a front or rear range of shops of the kind usual in Romano-British *fora* and their depths, 7.3 m (24 ft) overall, are virtually the same as the ones at the front of the *forum* at Caerwent. Identification of the building as a *forum* is confirmed by its breadth. At a minimum of 70 m for the shops, it is considerably wider than Caerwent and somewhat wider than Silchester. If the drain traversing the range recorded by Ecroyd Smith is contemporary with it, then we are probably entitled to infer the presence of a colonnaded courtyard behind the shops with inward-sloping roofing and drains taking the rain-water. The former will then have faced north, but since Romano-British *fora* box the compass, this is not significant. No evidence, epigraphic or otherwise, for the details of the administration of the *civitas* of the Brigantes has survived at their tribal centre.

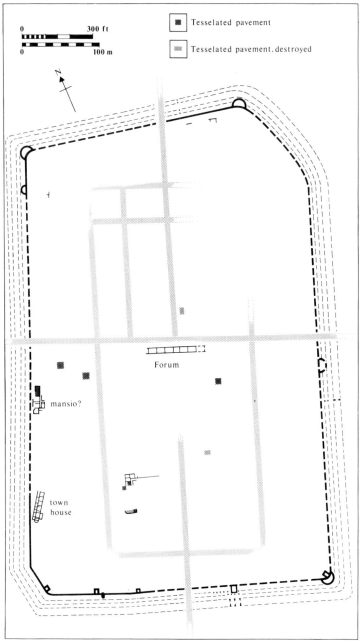

Fig.14. Plan of Aldborough (Isurium Brigantum).

One very weathered inscription built into the church at Kirby Hill a mile and a half from Aldborough, must be from the town and records a posthumous dedication *Divo Antonino (Magno?)*. This must be an official stone, presumably erected by decree of the *ordo*, probably to Caracalla who will have visited Aldborough, rather than Antoninus Pius, who did not. It also explicitly involves the imperial cult in the guise of the *Domus Divina* or Imperial household.[23]

One other building, inside the western defences south of the gate, excavated in 1830, has tentatively been suggested as a *mansio*. It is not clear whether the bath-suite is part of a *mansio*, as John Wacher has suggested, or whether it belonged to an opulent private house. The fragmentary plan hints at a verandahed courtyard which could equally fit either type of building and an appeal to size alone will not settle the identification, since large private houses existed at Isurium. If we could be sure that the tesselated passage flanked by two column bases between the baths and the gate was associated, however, then interpretation as a *mansio* would become more likely.[24]

We should expect Isurium to have had a public bathhouse, perhaps a theatre, and an amphitheatre, as well as temples. None is attested, except the latter by impli-cation of reliefs. Nor can we say anything of an aqueduct, though tanks for collecting roof water existed at three of the gates. If the authorities of the *civitas* followed the normal pattern, they would have seen to the completion of all public buildings and of the street-grid before turning their minds to the enclosure of the town by 'defences.' At Aldborough, as the late Miss Charlesworth has shown, a ditch was cut and an earthen bank was constructed at some date after A.D.150, but before A.D.200.[25] We do not know whether the gates going with it were of timber or stone. The latter is by no means impossible on analogy elsewhere.[26] At Aldborough it is normally assumed that the early bank follows the same circuit as the town wall. Estimates of the precise date obviously depend on whether it is felt that such banks and ditches appeared simultaneously all over Britain in response to a general crisis, such as that postulated for the later 190s, or whether one regards the appearance of 'defences' as an individual civic affair.

There now seems to be no doubt that the town wall was added in front of the original bank in the third century. It is of red sandstone and varies in thickness from 2.5 m (*c.* 8 ft) to just over 3 m (*c.* 10 ft), which suggests the probability of gangs building to different standards, as happened elsewhere. An interesting feature of the new defences is that interval towers are attested as contemporary with the wall, though so far they are only known on the southern defences.[27] Presumably the towers were copied from the standard second-century military practice (perhaps because military engineers were involved in the work) and their assistance may hint that the town wall was built before the late third century, as were those at Cirencester, Verulamium, London and the *coloniae*. The towers were evidently filled with sand to the level of the rampart. The best evidence of date for the wall remains a coin, thought to belong to the Severan house and incorporated in the footings when very worn. A date after A.D.230 therefore seems likely.[28] No useful details of the contemporary gates are known. The reason for the addition of the wall can only be conjectured, but it would not be surprising if the second-century bank was continually eroding and needed a front support.

The final stages of the town's defences are clearly much more military in their nature, since bastions were added over the inner ditch once it had been filled. This implies the use of mounted artillery, professional weapons requiring trained gun crews and technicians. Six bastions are known so far, all built at least partly in Millstone Grit, three of which, massive and semi-circular or semi-elliptical, at the angles of the town projected some 9 m (29.5 ft). The internal towers, which were less massive and projected about 5.5 m (18 ft), presumably survived in use. It is clear that the bastion at the northwest corner was added in the fourth century, probably not earlier than about A.D.320. Whether the Aldborough modernization is to be connected with the Theodosian restoration of A.D.369, which is often invoked to explain such additions, has to remain uncertain. A break in the east wall just north of the southeast corner has been repaired with a patch of masonry, including Millstone Grit blocks which the excavators thought came from the corner bastion. The implied date of reconstruction would be in the later fourth century or later, but the circumstances leading to the need for repairs are totally unknown.

The only other general feature of the town needing comment is the streets. Recent aerial photographs have shown that the central area was laid out in a grid, though there is not enough evidence yet to allow generalisations about the sizes of the *insulae* (Fig. 14).

For houses in the town we have to rely virtually entirely on antiquarian accounts summarized in a confusing manner by Ecroyd Smith.[29] While almost all details of chronological development escape us, two points emerge firmly, namely that there was an extraordinary abundance of mosaics, mainly of a geometrical nature; secondly that some of the houses were large and must surely have belonged to decurions of the *civitas*. At present the evidence for both mosaics and large houses falls largely in the southern part of the town, though this may be accidental and related to development of the village over the last two hundred years.

As an example of what must have been a major town house, we may consider the larger structure with an apsidal room in the southwestern quarter. The length of the recorded part over the walls is 16 m (52.5 ft); internally it is divided into a small room with mosaic 3 m (*c.* 10 ft) by 7.5 m (*c.* 24.5 ft), a large room 6.7 m (*c.* 22 ft) long and a 7.5 m (*c.* 24.5 ft) wide off which opens an apse with a radius of 3.9 m (*c.* 13 ft), a series of columns or pillars dividing the two. In the apse is a fragmentary mosaic with Greek inscriptions naming Mount Helicon, thought to portay the nine Muses, including Clio with a scroll(?).[30] In a private house the larger room and apse should be the *triclinium*, and the size here seems perfectly adequate. The subject at least suggests an awareness of classical themes, though the mosaic may, of course, have been selected from a pattern book. If one connects the group of rooms with a hypocausted range around a porticoed court 12.3 m (*c.* 40.5 ft) further north, then the eventual building would be some 46 m (*c.* 151 ft) long in one direction, thus putting it in the category of some of the larger town houses of Roman Britain. Of lesser buildings, such as shops and workshops, little is known, though Ecroyd Smith records one, apparently with grooved stones to take shutters, immediately west of the supposed *forum*.[31]

The town has produced only two tombstones, neither particularly informative, though one involves a woman whose husband was apparently a Roman citizen. Her own name was Felicula which was commonly servile.[32] The cemeteries themselves are scarcely more useful. Some cremation took place immediately outside the southwest corner of the town, as did inhumations, and some eighteen skeletons were found including one with a coin in the mouth.[33] The so-called 'red graves' outside the southeast corner appear to be furnaces of some kind, but they are not necessarily connected with cremation. Ecroyd Smith believed that burial was normally carried out outside the northwest corner of the town.

Of the gates, the south one led to York, the north to Catterick, but there seems to have been a by-pass around the north of the town. The west gate no doubt took the Ilkley road, the east gate possibly a link with Thornton-le-Street.

Colonia Eboracensis

The normal pattern was for a legionary fortress to have *canabae*, literally 'huts,' around it leased by the legion to civil traders and the families of serving soldiers. Such a settlement is well attested at York. Analogy on the Continent would suggest that a separate civil town, not part of the legion's land, would tend to grow up at some distance from the fortress, as at Nijmegen, Xanten, Carnuntum and Aquincum, to name some of the best-attested examples. At York the comparable civil settlement is not far distant, but is separated from the fortress by the River Ouse. As long as it was not chartered, this settlement would presumably fall to the jurisdiction of the *civitas*. Even when it was chartered it was still of vital importance to the *civitas* as the main port of external trade and so it cannot be entirely neglected here.

It is clear that the settlement had been granted colonial status by A.D.237 and it is perhaps likely to have achieved that status under Caracalla to mark his accession at York on the death of his father in February 211.[34] However, Aurelius Victor describes Eboracum as a *municipium* at the time of Severus's death.[35] If he was correct we have no means of judging when York was granted its municipal status. It is unlikely that the town, even when chartered, had a *territorium* since the grants would be virtually honorary titles and, if the *territorium legionis* still existed, it is difficult to see how such a *territorium* could have been assigned to the town.

Little can be said about the origins of the civil settlement. It was presumably named Eburacum like the fortress. In later times it seems to have been known as Colonia Eboracensis. Such buildings as are recorded for it, with one or two exceptions investigated recently, are largely known from nineteenth-century records and have no dating evidence. It might be expected that the earliest development would be along the line of the York-Tadcaster road. However, the earliest buildings for which we have evidence are sufficiently distant from the road both to the north and to the south to suggest otherwise. On the north side, underneath the later bath building discovered when the old station was built (Fig. 15,3), were some timber structures apparently of the late first or early second century.[36] To the south not far from the Ouse in Fetter Lane was a substantial stone building incorporating a plunge bath 2.8 m (*c.* 9 ft) wide by at least 7.4 m (*c.* 24 ft) long, as well as two other large rooms. This was clearly part of a bathhouse and the sizes of the rooms imply a public rather than a private one (Fig. 15,2). The date is almost certainly early in the history of the site since one of the rooms, 6.5 m (*c.* 21.5 ft) wide, had a floor of tiles which carried the stamp LEG IX HIS.[37] To these we may now add the presence of pre-Antonine timber buildings close to the bridge over the Ouse. Instead of ribbon development along the Tadcaster road, the position of these sites suggests a substantial area of development well beyond it to both the north and south, though it is unlikely that the development would have exceeded a distance of 280 m (*c.* 920 ft) from the river if the tombstone of the legionary standard-bearer L. Duccius Rufinus was in its original position when found at Holy Trinity, Micklegate.[38] Development of the later second century is known at

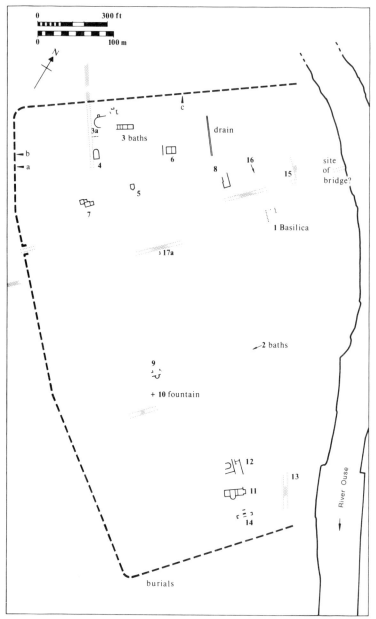

Fig.15.   Plan of the *colonia* at York (Colonia Eboracensis).

Bishophill Senior, where a single rectangular building has produced evidence of working in bronze and, perhaps, iron at that date (Fig. 15,11). Such activity may have been on the fringe of the town.

Evidence for development of a street grid is minimal. But there was a second road parallel to the road from Tadcaster to the bridge-head, but curiously enough only 37 m (c. 121.5 ft) away from it.[39] The intervening space could hardly have been divided into *insulae* in the conventional way. Elsewhere there are slight hints of roads parallel or at right angles to the main street; as Herman Ramm has observed, the mediaeval street system may preserve the Roman one in part, though with considerable distortion. Evidence for a rigid grid of streets is therefore largely lacking at York.[40]

It has been usual to assume that the civil town was defended with a wall and presumably a ditch which on the northern side largely lay under the Dark Age bank. There is a wall underneath this bank in places and on *a priori* grounds one might expect it to be Roman in date. However, its presence at specific points does not necessarily mean that it followed the line of the mediaeval defences everywhere, and it has long been pointed out that the Baile Hill area is likely to have been outside the town on the strength of burials with stamped tiles of Legio VI.[41] Furthermore, the nineteenth-century records imply that the wall diverged from the course of the mediaeval bank before the latter turned towards Micklegate Bar (Fig. 15,a-b), though the precise direction is left vague and John Wacher's recent comment on the relationship of the possible street grid to the defences should perhaps be treated cautiously.[42] In this century the wall has only once been recorded, in a tunnel opposite to the present railway station (Fig. 15,c). The published profile looks remarkably un-Roman in character, but an unpublished photograph shows us why. What was recorded was the mortar-and-rubble core of the wall, from which almost all the facing stones have gone. However, a few survive on the inner face, which had at least four courses of small, squared stones similar to those in the late defences of the fortress. Furthermore, an unpublished section shows what looks very much like the construction trench for the wall, cutting sandy material which was apparently based on decayed wood. In other words, it seems virtually certain that the wall was cut into an existing bank. The wall must be Roman, and its thickness, about 10 Roman feet, shows that it cannot have belonged to a building. We must, therefore, accept it as defensive, whether a refurbishing of existing defences or not. However, there is still the problem of the presence of Roman inhumations, including at least one gypsum burial, within the line of the wall and possible bank. On the face of it these ought to imply a date later than A.D. 300 for both bank, if it existed, and wall. However, there may possibly be some special explanation for them. The precise date of the wall is completely open, and the area that it enclosed is not much more certain, though a minimum estimate gives 18 ha (45 acres) and the maximum would be less than 24 ha (60 acres). As always, the area enclosed is not necessarily significant, and we have much evidence at York for both extramural houses and industrial activity. No wall has yet appeared on the river front, and one would be unlikely, initially at least.[43]

For public buildings within the *colonia*, details of chronology are for the most part sadly lacking, and it is usual to assume that major building activity was confined to the third century or later, when substantial buildings are assumed to have appeared. This, however, is only an assumption. As we have already seen, there is reason to think that a public bathhouse was at Fetter Lane much earlier. Excavation in 1939 near the Old Station clearly demonstrates an early complexity of building there, and certainly comparable activity is hinted at elsewhere inside the *colonia*.[44] Within the enclosed area, land was apparently at a premium, since four terraces, the uppermost of the third century, cut into the natural clay and revetted by stone walls 1 m (*c.* 3 ft) thick and about 2 m (*c.* 6.5 ft) high, are clear attempts to provide improved property for building purposes on the hill-slope between the river and Bishophill Senior (Fig. 15,13). Though as yet there is little evidence to suggest that the project was city-wide rather than local, it nonetheless is probable that such urban development included the destruction of older buildings.[45]

Among the public structures usually associated with the civil settlement are those connected with Imperial government. As York was the capital of Britannia Inferior in the third century, it has sometimes been thought that a governor's palace should exist at that date in or near the town. However, since the office of governor coincided with the command of Legio VI, the legate presumably used his *praetorium* in the fortress as his civil headquarters. After the Diocletianic reforms, when civil and military power were separated and Britain formed a diocese split into four provinces, a *praetorium* should have been provided for the governor of the new province governed from York (whether Britannia Secunda or Flavia Caesarensis). That presumably will have been somewhere on the south bank of the Ouse. Furthermore, claims have been made for a palace built for Severus and Julia Domna. No structure can be so identified and nothing in the written records compels us to believe that one existed at York. The rescript in the *Corpus Iuris* for A.D.210 (*Cod. Iur.* iii 32,7) was issued at York, and Severus of course died there, so it was probably his northern headquarters while in Britain, but in all probability Severus used the *praetorium* of the fortress as his headquarters and residence.[46] The presence of Julia Domna or Geta would not alter the matter, and it is most unlikely that there would have been time to build a fitting imperial residence.

Just inside the northern defences of the *colonia*, in the area of the Old Station, a complicated series of buildings, some or all bathhouses, have been recorded. The best known is a fragmentary structure with oversized walls ending to the southwest in a buttressed apse, probably part of a hot room (Fig. 15,3a). A similar buttressed wall, possibly also with an apse, lies between 18.5 m (*c.* 60.5 ft) and 31 m (*c.* 102 ft) further northeast. These were clearly part of a major public building and are usually, and probably correctly, considered to be part of a bathhouse, though the evidence is not quite conclusive. It overlies fragments of earlier buildings, at least one of timber and two of stone construction. The probable bathhouse is approximately parallel to the main street through the *colonia* leading to the bridge over the Ouse. It is thought to be third-century.[47]

On a different and probably earlier alignment, lying 31 m (*c.* 102 ft) east of the centre of the apse of the last building, was another series of rooms with two plunge baths separated by two unheated rooms equal in size (Fig. 15,3). The better-preserved plunge was about 4.5 m (*c.* 15 ft) square. Apparently associated with this building is a small square structure which yielded an altar to Fortuna trimmed for use as a building stone (*RIB* 644). This building is again much more likely to be part of a public bathhouse rather than a private bath-suite.[48]

About 62 m (*c.* 203.5 ft) east of the last building, and so scarcely part of it, was another on the same alignment, again including a plunge bath this time measuring 9 m (29.5 ft) × 4.6 m (*c.* 15 ft) (Fig. 15,36). A rather large, cold room separated it from a hypocaust furnace of unusual tiled construction. Again the scale of the building suggests public use.[49]

While these baths were clearly not contemporary, taking the Fetter Lane bath into account as well, York seems unusually well-endowed with such buildings for a British town.[50]

Another building of importance, located nearer the river and excavated in 1898, possessed two parallel rows of columns 12.2 m (40 ft) apart (Fig. 15,1). In each the columns were massive, 1 m (*c.* 3 ft) in diameter, and were 2 m (*c.* 6.5 ft) apart. The larger row had seven columns, the shorter only four, while an intervening column stood equidistant between the two rows at one end.[51] If the last column was in position the resultant form, that of an aisled building, is similar to the familiar Vitruvian basilica often associated with Roman *fora* though a column on the long axis would be a solecism. The recorded dimensions suggest a great hall 25 m (82 ft) wide and the diameters of the columns imply that they stood about 9 m (29.5 ft) high. The choice of the Vitruvian form of *basilica* may imply the presence of a gallery over the aisles and their returns at each end of the hall. It is difficult to explain a basilican hall on this scale as anything but part of a *forum* and *basilica*. Since there is not room to fit in the conventional colonnaded court surrounded by shops between the hall and the river, the putative *forum* should have faced the other way. Its relationship to road 17a is uncertain.

If that road existed as a coherent whole from Micklegate Bar to Barker Lane, the suggested *forum* would have cut across its projected line. But the building could not have been centred on the road, as that would mean a total width of about 50 m (164 ft), which would be ridiculously narrow, since the length of the basilica alone should be well over 62 m (*c.* 203.5 ft), if it had normal proportions. Interestingly enough, this same site produced a fragmentary altar dedicated to the *numen* of the Emperor and to a *genius*, probably the *Genius* of Eboracum.[52] Such an inscription would be likely to be official and would be particularly appropriate in the *forum* of the city.

Of other buildings in the public or semi-public domain, only temples may be inferred from the surviving evidence, though none has been recorded structurally. The existence of a college of *Augustales* at York, attested by two inscriptions, implies a temple or shrine of the Imperial cult, perhaps most likely to have been associated with the *forum*.[53] A Serapeum is directly attested by an early third-century dedicatory inscription set up by the governor of Lower Britain and found in the *colonia* underneath an apsed building near Barker Lane (Fig. 15,15). The temple had presumably been demolished by the fourth century.[54] Two Mithraic sculptures from the *colonia* demonstrate the presence of at least one temple of that cult.[55] A recent inscription attests another temple, perhaps extramural, for which an arch and possibly an entrance passage were provided by a merchant from northern Gaul (p. 107). The whereabouts of the Christian cathedral is unknown, though it must have existed by A.D.314 since Eborius *episcopus de civitate Eburacensi* attended the Council of Arles in that year. As Frere has observed, Christianity would be likely to have spread fastest in the cosmopolitan society of large ports and cities. Nor would Constantine's association with York have discouraged such a growth in the town. There is at least one Christian inscription from a burial, *soror ave vivas in deo*, even if the burial itself was not Christian. Furthermore, as will be noted below, the late inhumations with gypsum may possibly be connected with Christianity. Indeed, the existence of further churches or cemetery chapels is to be expected, one perhaps outside the fortress in the vicinity of the Castle

Yard. Nothing is known in detail of the public water supply, though its existence is implied at York. There would have been a piped supply to public bathhouses and also to fountains, one of which is known from Bishophill Junior in the *colonia* (Fig. 15,10).[56]

The most notable of private houses is one on Toft Green which had at least five rooms, three with mosaics having parallels at Aldborough.[57] The surviving fragments suggest a house around a courtyard rather than anything else (Fig. 15,7). Other substantial houses clearly existed at Tanner Row, one perhaps a corridor house with slightly projecting wings (Fig. 15,8),[58] and another of the Toft Green buildings is notable for an apsidal room floored with a particularly fine mosaic depicting a sea cow (Fig. 15,5).[59] Recent work on Bishophill has added two buildings, one certainly, the other probably, domestic, adjacent to each other and set on one of the artificial terraces made in the late second or early third century. Despite their proximity they are aligned rather differently. The smaller, and certainly domestic, building was elaborated in the fourth century and given an apsed room, perhaps a *triclinium* (Fig. 15,11). It and two other rooms, and a corridor, were all heated by hypocausts, but the arrangement cannot be interpreted as a bath-suite. One wing was largely excavated and appears to have been joined by the heated corridor to another parallel wing.[60] The adjacent building (Fig. 15,12) looks as if it began life as a courtyard house after construction of the terrace, but it seems to have been demolished in the early fourth century, and it was perhaps then that a building with apses and hypocausts was inserted in the former courtyard. This is most likely to have been a bath-suite of another house. Its scale precludes a public nature.[61]

Another building in the *colonia* at St Mary Bishophill Junior, is likely to have been built in the late third or early fourth century (Fig. 15,9). Originally domestic, it once more had an added apse subsequently enlarged. The associated finds, including a Theodosian coin, go down to the end of the century. In its final phase, the building had a large deposit of bones of herring and sprats immediately over-lying its floor. This strongly suggests the probability that it had become a manufactory of fish sauce of the kind known as *garum*.[62]

If the usual assumptions about the defences around the town are correct, then it is clear that there was much extramural building which included substantial houses. Two known in the vicinity of Micklegate Bar, one with a mosaic floor, probably lay outside the *colonia* wall.[63] Another, however, existed at Clementhorpe east of the *colonia* and not far from the river. There was some second-century occupation in the area but a substantial house is only attested for the fourth century. The fragments recovered suggest a corridor house facing east, or possibly a courtyard house. It had mosaic floors and one room, some 7.7 m × 9.2 m (*c*. 25 ft × 30 ft), had a polygonal apse added to it.[64]

It is evident that by the fourth century, at the latest, York had a considerable number of houses with mosaic floors and with apses. The latter are indeed strikingly frequent there and hardly less so at Aldborough. This treatment presumably reflects the social style of the well-to-do in the area in the later Roman period. The current fad of adding bow-windows during the 'restoration' of country cottages in Yorkshire comes to mind as a parallel.

The town at York is fortunate in having two large Roman cemeteries, one discovered in the 1870s when the Railway Station was built, the other at Trentholme Drive southwest of the road to Tadcaster excavated recently. In a sense these two cemeteries are complementary, since the one has an abundance of grave-goods implying that it belonged to the relatively wealthy section of the community, but was ill-recorded. The other has rather meagre objects accompanying the burials but was fully recorded and has fascinating evidence of the longevity of the poorer inhabitants. In addition to these two, there is evidence for individual *mausolea* of the richest members of York society along the line of the Tadcaster and Aldborough roads. Although stone coffins are relatively common in many areas of Britain, inscribed *sarcophagi* intended for use in *mausolea* are comparatively rare and York has a remarkable wealth of them. They are clearly related to high social status and include coffins of a decurion, the wife of a decurion, a *sevir Augustalis* and his wife, and a centurion's daughter.[65] An interesting sidelight on York is that many of these *sarcophagi* were desecrated and reused for inhumations. Removal of such massive objects called for team work and must have been condoned, if not sanctioned, by authority. The possibility that such desecration was done at the hands of Christians is not to be dismissed out of hand; some of the *sarcophagi* were reused for that other interesting class of burials which is well-attested at York, namely those in gypsum, which are often seen as Christian.[66] About 50 sarcophagi have been recorded, mostly from cemeteries associated with the town. The use of lead coffins was also relatively common at York with more than fourteen attested.[67] There seems to be some evidence from the old records for common burials of the poorest class of inhabitants,[68] but most of the burials of the less affluent were in individual graves, with or without wooden coffins. The Trentholme Drive cemetery, which is composed entirely of poor burials, suggests that at this level the average expectation of life of those who had survived infancy was about 40 years.[69] Furthermore, it produced some evidence suggesting that the women belonged to one basic, presumably indigenous, type; the male skeletons were more varied and included some with eastern or African characteristics.[70]

Finally, before leaving York, the last point serves as a reminder that we are dealing with a cosmopolitan community with widespread connexions with other parts of the empire, whether in the origin of individuals, or in the trading connexions which existed with other provinces (p. 105).

Catterick and Corbridge

The remaining two towns to be discussed have different backgrounds from Aldborough and York. Catterick, the site of a Flavian fort held down to about A.D.125, and then again from about A.D.160, was for much of its life simply a *vicus* attached to the fort. Ptolemy names it as Cataractonium, a name which is thought to refer to the rapids in the Swale, possibly from a Celtic word cognate with the Latin *cataracta*.

Others suggest derivation from a Celtic word *catura(c)tonium* 'battle-ramparts', referring to the Roman fort.[71] Towards the end of the third century or early in the fourth century, the *vicus* and fort were unified and surrounded by a free-standing wall seven and one-half feet wide, fronted by a very large ditch and enclosing 6 ha (15.5 acres).[72] This clearly implies a very different state of affairs from the normal *vicus* by that time, and the comparison that should be made is with southern and midland towns developing in the Flavian period from the *vici* of forts recently abandoned. It seems likely that at this stage Catterick was given a more regular grid of streets than was usual in small Romano-British towns (Fig. 16).

Little is known of the earliest *vicus* at Catterick since the area excavated in 1958–1959 lay immediately east of the fort, and it appears to have been given over to the working of leather on a large scale, presumably by the army.[73] After the evacuation of the fort by Hadrian, a *mansio* was established around the former bathhouse, which was rebuilt to serve it.

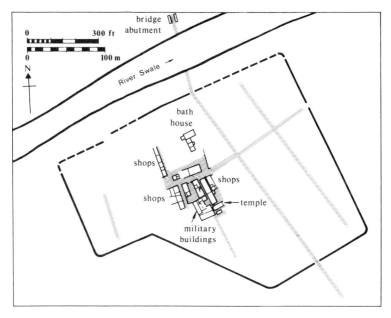

Fig.16.   Plan of Catterick (Cataractonium) in the 4th century.

An associated inscription of a cohors IX implies legionary building.[74] However, while occupation of the area south of the Swale seems to have been confined entirely to the *mansio*, a new site appeared under Hadrian, or slightly later, north of the river around the bridgehead, and straddling Dere Street. It had a narrow turf rampart enclosing about four and one-half acres and four widely spaced ditches, though it was probably open along the river bank. Nothing is known of internal buildings.[75] This enigmatic site is scarcely a normal auxiliary fort, though its command of Dere Street and the bridgehead is suggestive of a desire to control or inspect traffic along the main road. It is perhaps unlikely to be simply paddocks associated with the *mansio* in view of its relationship to the road.

Unfortunately, it is not known when the auxiliary fort at Catterick was finally given up. That timber buildings had appeared during the course of the second century along the street leading east from the fort is clear, but the excavations were confined to an area west of Dere Street between it and the fort, and so nothing is known of what was happening along the main road to the north. In the third century it seems that the *mansio* had been abolished and that stone shops replaced the earlier ones. They were in the main simple rectangular buildings with open fronts (of a kind often called strip-houses), though a *podium* suggests a temple. There is evidence of a contemporary aqueduct feeding a fountain. Rebuilding about the time the town wall appeared was evidently extensive in the excavated area, but an attempt to refurbish the bathhouse of the former *mansio* was abandoned. No doubt a public bath existed elsewhere within the town in the third century. Further rebuilding is dated to the period around A.D.370 when many of the shops had their fronts walled up. John Wacher also makes a case for the appearance at this time of a military enclave in the town (see p. 114). The bridgehead site north of the Swale seems to have developed into a suburb of the town by the early fourth century. It included at least one temple and shops were evidently present by the late fourth century.[76] The vicinity of the temple has produced a clay ritual mask. (Fig. 17) with projections at the top which served to suspend it, as

Fig.17.   A ritual mask from Catterick, (c. ½).

they are pierced by transverse holes, but which may also remind us of the horns attested for at least one Brigantian god (p. 10–11 with Fig. 4).[77]

Like Catterick, the Roman site at Corbridge is at the crossing of a major river (the Tyne), but this time it lies on the north bank. There is some considerable doubt about the Roman name of the site. The familiar form Corstopitum, derived from the Antonine Itinerary, is not Celtic, and the name Corielopocarium which appears in the Ravenna Cosmography may be nearer the truth, though perhaps itself corrupt, like so many names in the Cosmography. Coriostopitum has recently been conjectured as another possibility.[78]

A series of forts which existed at Corbridge in the period down to A.D.163 or so no doubt attracted considerable civil settlement, but the most recent excavations of the site have mainly been concerned with the central area occupied initially by the forts and little is known of the early civil elements. Once the auxiliary forts were given up there was a greater possibility for civil development despite the fact that Corbridge retained some military installations down to the fourth century. Such a development of civilian and soldier mingling in the same site is of course most unusual in the western provinces before the late fourth century, and it adds

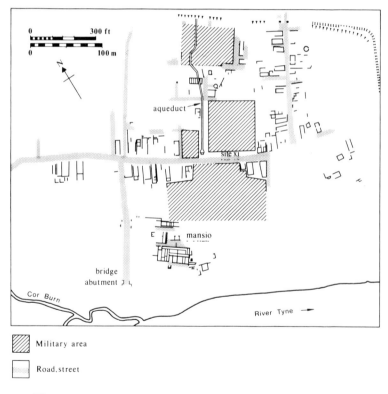

Fig.18.   Plan of Corbridge (Coriosopitum or Coriolopocarium?).

greatly to the interest of Corbridge (Fig. 18). The familiar problem of dating the civilian structures inevitably comes to the fore since most of them were excavated before 1914. Nevertheless, it is quite clear that temples had appeared along the south edge of the east–west street before the building of the military compounds for legionaries operating a metal-working depot.[79] The temples stand out immediately as being something quite different from the normal Romano-British tradition. Some of them are rustic versions of the Graeco-Roman pedimented temple set on a platform or *podium*. The form chosen was no doubt influenced by the backgrounds of the soldiers quartered at the site. Presumably the cults in question were supported largely by the soldiers, but the very existence of the temples in such large numbers presupposes a sizeable civilian body of worshippers. As for the rusticity of the temples, at least one involves the architectural solecism of a portico of five columns. Assuming that the unfinished store building, Site XI, is second-century rather than later, it is perhaps unlikely that any part of it would have been given over to civilian affairs at that time, and we are left without any non-religious public buildings.

At some stage the front range of Site XI seems to have been completed in slighter masonry than the original intentions, and it appears that a portico was added along the main east–west street; presumably shops are in question.[80] For the rest, the civilian buildings at Corbridge seem to be very largely the familiar rectangular structures set at right angles to the street. While few have any evidence of internal division, sometimes this will have been by timber partitioning. The evidence for the use of a second floor with such buildings, demonstrated for Dacia by Trajan's column,[81] does not necessarily have to apply in Britain, though it would perhaps be surprising if the loft-space was not used for providing sleeping accommodation for servants and workmen. The buildings clearly combined the functions of shops, workshops and living quarters in many instances, though some were no doubt purely domestic, and others will have served as inns, cookshops and the like. Unfortunately, it is virtually impossible from the older accounts of the excavations to decide the dates of most of the buildings, which could belong to any period from the later second to the fourth centuries, and it is accordingly difficult to say anything of the development of the town. However, in its final phase there must have been something of the order of 80 to 100 of the rectangular buildings, spread over at least 18 ha (44 acres) (which, however, also includes the military installations), and this probably implies a civilian population of at least 800.[81a] It is also clear that there was some attempt at producing a more-or-less regular street grid with most of the buildings known set at right angles to either the main east–west street, or the one joining it at right angles in the eastern part of the town leading to what appears to have been the north gate.

In the southwest quarter of the town, south of the military compounds installed to provide a metal-working depot, is a large elaborate building of several phases of construction. This has usually been identified as a *mansio*, no doubt correctly, though it could be argued that the building is even more elaborate than has been suggested hitherto, since the adjacent building (Site III) could be regarded as an opposite wing providing more accommodation around a courtyard. Another building at right angles to the two blocks is simpler in nature and could be taken as the western range of the same complex.[82] Though the area in question has a complicated history, as two underlying structures of unknown function suggest, the advantage of this interpretation is that it would make the Corbridge building of much the same size as the comparable one detected from the air at Chesters.[83] Otherwise the Corbridge *mansio* would be surprisingly small for such an important centre.

The eighteenth-century antiquaries were quite clear that Corbridge had been walled, and there is firm evidence for a ditch and bank in the northwestern corner of the site, probably with a stone wall at the front of the bank. There is also some evidence of gates both at the Tyne bridgehead and on the north side of the town. The date of the defences, however, is uncertain, though obviously unlikely to be earlier than the third century. If they involved a contemporary wall and bank, it is in the provision of these defences, as well as in its size, some 18 ha (44 acres), that Corbridge differs from the other northern *vici*. It is open to question, however, whether it had any administrative responsibilities as a *pagus* centre for the hypothetical Lopocares (see p. 1). The absence of any obvious *forum* is worrying.

The surviving civilian inscriptions, few in number, suggest a cosmopolitan population. An altar to Herakles in Greek is dedicated by a high priestess (*RIB* 1129), and there is another in Greek to Astarte (*RIB* 1124). A Palmyrene merchant, who appears to have been involved in supplying flags to the army, represents the east (*RIB* 1171 to be taken with his wife's epitaph from South Shields *RIB* 1065), and a young girl whose name is given in a German diminutive form will have had at least one parent of that nationality (*RIB* 1180). We are left with two civilian inscriptions in which the names give no clues to the origin and one which appears to be Celtic (*RIB* 1181). The position of the Corbridge cemeteries seems to be unrecorded, and the tombstones noted above were mainly reused in either Roman or later structures. Only one found east of the town is likely to have been near its original position (*RIB* 1174). The mausoleum west of the town on Shorden Brae is unlikely to have anything to do with the civilian population and is much more probably the tomb of a senior military man.[84]

Minor Settlements

Within the area of the *civitas* there was a very large number of minor settlements, mostly existing side by side with auxiliary forts, though some few continued to exist after evacuation of the forts, or probable forts, as at Adel.[85] Settlements apparently totally divorced from the military network are rare, and very few have been investigated at all. As examples of this, we might instance Wetherby,[86] or possibly Tadcaster,[87] though the latter may have had its origin in a fort of the 70s, later replaced by Newton Kyme. But again and again one comes back to the *vici* attached to the forts as the places showing the highest level of romani-

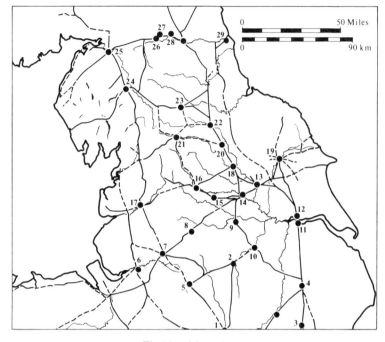

Fig.19.   Map of *vici*.
Sites within Brigantia with substantial evidence for *vici*:

1 Little Chester	2 Templeborough	5 Buxton
6 Wilderspool	7 Manchester	8 Slack
9 Castleford	10 Doncaster	14 Tadcaster
15 Adel	16 Ilkley	17 Ribchester
20 Healam Bridge	21 Bainbridge	23 Bowes
26 Chesterholm	27 Housesteads	28 Chesters
29 South Shields		

zation and as the centres of local marketing (Fig. 19). As we
shall see subsequently, not a few of these produce evidence
of industrial activity, too. Comparatively little is known of
their early development, though here and there inscriptions, as at Templeborough or Ilkley, attest *vici* before
Hadrian, and the presence of Dobunnic and Cornovian
women respectively (*RIB* 621, 639). In fact, civilian
settlements will have begun to appear outside all the forts as

soon as they were founded. At first the buildings will have
been simple timber ones, as at Slack where ribbon development along the road from Chester to York took place in the
Flavian period (Fig. 20), and where many of the huts had
been rebuilt more than once before the abandonment of the
site at the evacuation of the fort around A.D.140.[88] This site

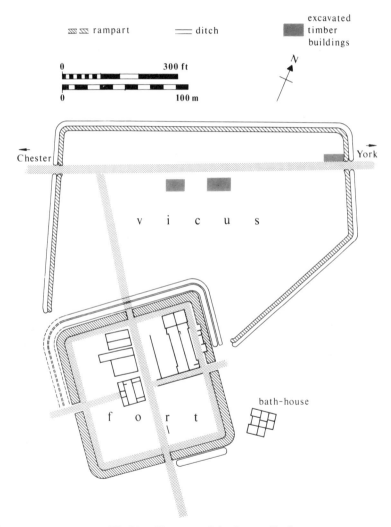

Fig.20.   The *vicus* of the fort at Slack.

is particularly interesting because already under Hadrian a
ditch and bank surrounded it and linked it to the fort. The
arrangement at Melandra, including defences, offers a close
parallel, but adds a timber *mansio* with a complicated plan,
perhaps not all of one construction.[89] The best known *vici*
are of course those associated with Hadrian's Wall, where
civilian development was initially excluded from the military zone defined by the Vallum. Almost nothing is known
of the Hadrianic *vici* except at Housesteads, where a few of
the Hadrianic timber buildings have been located south of
the Vallum.[90] Building in stone is known at Chesterholm in
the mid-Antonine period and that became the norm for the
later *vici* which clustered around the forts once the Vallum
was out of commission. Regular planning of such *vici* is not
to be expected and clearly did not normally happen. Nor is
enclosure of the civilian buildings usual, though as we have
seen already it was used at Melandra and Slack in the
second century, and it also occurred at Bainbridge in the
later Roman period.[91] But at such isolated sites it is not
surprising. Other substantial *vici* in the hinterland of Hadrian's Wall which merit mention are those at Binchester,
Piercebridge and Greta Bridge, where the publication of the
recent work should add considerably to our knowledge. In
the settlements at sites like Chesters, or Housesteads, strip
buildings are dominant and must have served as shops,
taverns and hostels, as well as houses for the families of
soldiers.[92]

Of more exalted buildings, *mansiones* can sometimes be
detected, and characteristically the sites have series of
temples often patronized by army personnel who tended to
leave more inscriptions than their civilian fellow-wor-
shippers. Civilian bathhouses, however, are not known and
the implication is clearly that the *vicani* were allowed to use
the fort bathhouses which were, of course, normally external. Details here escape us, but the presumption must be
that certain hours were set aside for civilian use, at
moderate charge.[93]

Administratively such *vici* were in a somewhat anomalous
position since, although nominally subject to the order of
the *civitas*, local fort commanders undoubtedly exercised

some measure of general supervision and seem to have acted as local magistrates (p. 22). What part the *ordo* of the *civitas* played in the *vici* is by no means clear, though it is certain that the *vici* had some autonomy, as *vicani* acted as corporate bodies under pairs of functionaries styled *vicomagistri*, who presumably acted in effect as village headmen and consulted with the local army commanders in matters of common interest, as well as dealing with the *ordo* at need.[94]

4

Rural Settlement

As we have seen, the pre-Roman pattern of settlement in Brigantia was entirely rural and basically dispersed. Nothing akin to southern *oppida* existed, unless it is permissible to argue that Stanwick shows the first stages of similar trends to the southern sites (p. 14). Even hill-forts occupied in the first century A.D. seem to have been rare, and almost all the pre-Roman population was scattered throughout innumerable farmsteads or hamlets of kinsmen. However, as aerial photography continues to demonstrate yearly, in some of the more fertile, lowland areas the fields associated with such sites are contiguous over considerable distances. This applies especially at present to the Magnesian Limestone strip from Doncaster, fringing the Vale of York on the west and continuing into Durham and also to the sands and gravels of Doncaster.[1] But recently similar sites have begun to appear on the Coal Measures to the west, where one rectangular enclosure with rounded corners at Rothwell has yielded a well of Roman date.[2] In the hills of the Pennines, settlement was much sparser and for those who do not know the area at first hand it will be as well to stress the vast areas of flat, inhospitable moorland between the major Dales. It is on the flanks of the Dales themselves that the settlements tend, in general, to occur. Similarly the low overall density of rural settlement on the Lancashire side of the Pennines obtrudes. This is perhaps more puzzling, though to some extent exacerbated by the density of modern houses and the considerable marshy tracts south of Lancaster in the Ormskirk area. However, Roman urban trends are minimal, too, and are confined entirely to the *vici* of forts. Even in the hill country, there are areas, particularly on the limestone of upper Wharfedale, around Grassington, where locally there are settlements and fields as dense as on the Magnesian Limestone, and that is probably a phenomenon of Roman date.[3] Similarly, on the Cumberland coastal plain there was extensive settlement of the area later assigned to the separate *civitas* of the Carvetii.[4] Inevitably one wonders about the extreme north-eastern area of the Brigantes south of the Tyne. In view of Professor Jobey's evidence for further north, it will be surprising if settlement was not considerable, but much will have gone in the urban sprawl east of Gateshead. What survives is summarised in a recent survey, which also produces evidence of cereals at several sites.[5]

None of the general points made so far give much evidence of a major Roman expansion within 'the most numerous *civitas* of the province' (Tacitus *Agr.* 17). More promising as a sign of Roman influence may be the regular 'brickwork' pattern of fields in some areas, notably near Doncaster (mainly, though not entirely, south of Rossington and so probably not Brigantian). Derrick Riley's valiant work on these from the air has been extremely valuable and needs to be followed up by more fieldwork, though some at least of the associated ditches have produced Roman pottery.[6]

The evident major outlay of a large tract of country east of Tadcaster with what seems to be an unusual type of centuriation is clear evidence of Roman reorganization.[7] Since Mr Ramm published his paper on it, aerial photography has added ditched native sites, aligned north-west to south-east with the trend of the contours, cut across by the system of Roman roads.[8] Here native holdings were swept away, and some degree of expropriation must have been involved. The system can have had nothing to do with the third-century *colonia* at York, and Mr Ramm's suggested late first-century dating is convincing. Public action is evident, and at that time it could scarcely be anybody but the Roman army that was responsible. Was this part of the legionary *territorum*, whether leased to native farmers or run by the army as its *prata?* The balance of probability is surely in favour of the latter and the distance from York need be no obstacle in view of analogies elsewhere.[9] However, its presence does serve to stress how unusual such arrangements were and also to remind us how little we know of what underlies the post-Roman silts of the Vale of York.

With exceptions such as that just noted, it seems likely that the arrival of the Roman army made little basic difference to native patterns of settlements and agriculture at first, though admittedly few of the settlements and field systems are securely dated. However, various factors would sooner or later begin to influence patterns of behaviour. Most important was the economic effect of the presence of the army with its large demands for grain, meat, lard, drink, hides, and timber.[10] This demand must have served to stimulate husbandry and production considerably and is likely to have affected cereal production in suitable areas. Furthermore, if the army involved itself in farming on the *prata legionis*, its methods and equipment would not go unnoticed by surrounding farmers. It is fashionable at present to play down Roman contribution to the development of British agriculture, and much is admittedly unclear, but to name only one major change of the Roman period, the introduction of the two-handed scythe must have increased the speed and efficiency of harvesting greatly. Even more vital was its importance in the hay harvest. For the first time an efficient means of cutting hay rapidly gave greater security to the vital winter feed. Those who remember the change in recent years from the old hay-time, with hay often lying in the meadows for weeks, to the modern, mechanized one will appreciate that the earlier change from use of small sickles was almost as vital.

It is clear that in many of the remoter settlements in the hills life went on in much the same fashion as it had before the coming of Rome. It is true that even there simple Roman goods would gradually filter in, as for instance in the Kildale area of the North Yorkshire Moors, though the convenience of a cash economy would not be strikingly obvious.[11] But, even the remotest settlements would eventually be affected by the new regime. On the adverse side were the taxes, including the tax in kind used for supporting the army, superimposed by the central government and by the *civitas* itself, which now had an expensive programme of building, maintenance and administration to support. But there were also gains, not least the ready and growing markets for farm products, both within Brigantia and the rest of the province, but also abroad (p. 103). The attendant *vici* of the Roman forts will have acted as the places of primary sale for those wishing to dispose of their wool, hides, cheese or any surplus grain. The *vici* apart, most settlements still tended to be scattered rather than nucleated.

Villas

While most of the sites discussed above are essentially continuing the pre-Roman practice of farming on a relatively small scale from isolated farmsteads or small hamlets, the Roman period saw the introduction of some more elaborate establishments with romanized houses divided into rooms set aside for particular purposes, and hence implying a more Roman way of life. These are the farming estates usually termed 'villas.' A distribution map of such sites in Britain makes it obvious that Brigantia was on the fringe of their development, and that their density where they do occur in the *civitas* is low compared to most of southern Britain.[12] It is in general clear that villa estates did not develop in the highland zone of Britain, and that they therefore tend to be missing from the areas under military control. However, we cannot argue that the absence of villas is due to the presence of the army, or even to the general absence of towns to act as central places for trade, since the *vici* associated with the forts could have performed that purpose just as well as towns. Another possible explanation for the absence of villas comes to mind, namely that the type of farming, being largely pastoral, did not give sufficient profit to build in the Roman manner. Against this must be urged that Brigantia as a whole was importing Roman goods, both from abroad and from southern Britain. Ultimately these would have had to be paid for in the main by the agricultural surpluses, hence there should have been considerable export of animal products from our area.

However, such profits as were gained would go largely to the merchants acting as middlemen rather than to the hill farmers. But even if there were profits sufficient to romanize farms, it seems highly likely that the hill folk were inately conservative and would not wish to do so. Evidently the same applied in those areas west of the Pennines which might be regarded as topographically more akin to the lowland zone. One apparent exception to the general rule of absence of villas in the Pennines is the site at Gargrave, near Skipton, but there are special geological conditions there, however, which explain its presence.

In the area east of the Pennines, mainly on the west flank of the Vale of York, we do have a considerable series of villas or probable villas which must be Brigantian. Nevertheless, even allowing for undiscovered sites there, the density will certainly always be lower than in Parisian lands (Fig. 21). One possible explanation is that it was usual for the larger land owners to live in the towns at York and Aldborough, both of which show signs of considerable numbers of wealthy houses. A social pattern of this kind has analogies elsewhere in Britain, particularly in the *civitates* of the Cornovii, the Dumnonii and the Silures.

A recent survey of villas in the north relates the distribution of Brigantian villas to York and Aldborough particularly.[13] In general this would perhaps be expected in view of the common pattern of relationships between towns and villas further south. However, there is quite certainly another factor to take into account in our area, namely the influence of geology and types of soil. Most of the villas west of the Vales of York and Mowbray are on the Magnesian Limestone, a fertile strip, which we have seen attracted dense settlement in the Iron Age. The two northernmost sites, at Holme House just south of the Tees, and at Old Durham, although close to the limestone, are on river gravels. With Gargrave in the upper Aire Valley we have a special case. There a former glacial lake left a large flat expanse of fertile soil. Loamy clays overlie the gravel of the old lake bed, giving a reasonably drained soil which nevertheless retains considerable moisture.

In his survey of northern villas, Branigan envisages

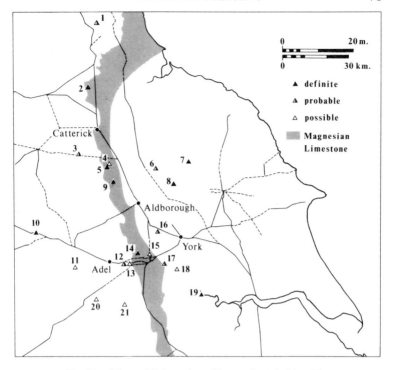

Fig.21. Map of Brigantian villas and probable villas.

Key:
1 Old Durham	8 Oulston	15 Moat House
2 Holme House	9 Castle Dykes	16 Wilstrop Hall
3 Middleham	10 Kirk Sink, Gargrave	17 Kirkby Wharfe
4 Snape	11 Gawthorpe	18 Cawood
5 Well	12 Biggin	19 Drax
6 Sutton	13 Scarcroft	20 Birstall
7 Beadlam	14 Dalton Parlours	21 Snapethorpe Hall

retired soldiers, merchants and Brigantian aristocracy as potential villa owners in that order of probability.[14] Since there is little precise evidence, it may be as well once more to consider the general pattern in Britain. One of the most striking phenomena in Romano-British studies in recent years has been the way in which excavations have again and again produced evidence either for pre-Roman or early

Roman farmsteads underlying or adjacent to villa houses. Furthermore, a pattern has also tended to emerge in Britain in which either gradual elaboration of houses, or the conversion of former barns partly or entirely into living quarters, or the addition of new houses, or a combination of these methods, appears to be the rule. Demonstration of ownership of sites from archaeological evidence is virtually impossible without specific inscriptions, of which there are few in Britain. The general pattern, however, does seem to be one of native land-owning families gradually acquiring wealth and investing it in structures. That is not to say, of course, that Roman officials, retired soldiers, immigrants to the province, or Romano-British merchants never founded or bought villa estates. But the impression gained is usually of continuity, with little hint of the kind of changes that one might expect if strangers took over. Surely, the same will have applied in Brigantia, where after all there was a strong philo-Roman element in the first century and where, despite problems with Rome, one would not expect natives who became members of the tribal council (*ordo*) to eschew Roman manners entirely on their countryside estates.

In Brigantia, there are only seven examples of definite villas, and a further six sites may be regarded as probable. There are other candidates which can only be relegated to the category 'possible' (Fig. 21).[15] The relation of the certain and probable villas to central places is rarely obvious, but tentative grouping for Aldborough is possible (Fig. 21). Others might be related to lesser centres like Adel, Newton Kyme or Tadcaster and Wetherby. Apart from the probable villa at Wilstrop, nothing obviously goes with York, but that of course could be because the Brigantian *curiales* favoured the Aldborough area. However, two further points need to be made, namely that the silts in the floor of the Vale of York could conceal some more romanized farms similar to Wilstrop, and certainly that the land division near Tadcaster, if truly a form of centuriation (p. 69), will have been connected initially with the York legion or, just possibly, later with the *municipium* and *colonia*.

Some generalities emerge for the better-known villas, particularly those excavated recently. As with some villas further south, like Winterton and Great Weldon, stone-built circular structures appear at Old Durham, and Holme House (Manfield).[16] They, perhaps, represent a halfway stage in romanization, despite clinging to the native plan for the houses. Gargrave (Kirk Sink) is at present the only site to have evidence of circular timber and turf-built houses, one of which survived in use into the villa period, though perhaps not then necessarily used as living quarters. For Dalton Parlours (Collingham) it has been stated that there is no continuity between the circular houses of the Iron Age and the third-century romanized buildings (cf. p. 85, however). But at the other sites, it seems as if romanization of the farms was normal in the second half of the second century. The initial romanized houses at Gargrave (Fig. 22, A) Dalton Parlours (Fig. 23), Beadlam and probably the partly destroyed one at Well are versions of the standard Romano-British villa house with front corridor and central entrance between slightly projecting wings. The three complete examples are all between 80 and 100 Roman feet (*pes monetalis*) in length, which is about the same as southern averages for houses of similar type.[17] The curious house at Drax, apparently with an initial timber phase, was replaced in stone probably in the third century and was a simple cottage house, later elaborated in a manner difficult to comprehend, and given an enclosed yard attached to its front.[18] At Gargrave and Dalton Parlours (Fig. 24) there were mosaic floors within the houses, and detached bathhouses occur at both sites; the one at Dalton Parlours was badly damaged by ploughing but was undoubtedly considerably larger than the obvious surviving rooms suggest. It had elaborate frescoes, including a decorated ceiling. Beadlam had no mosaic in the house and if there was a bathhouse it has not yet been found. But whereas Gargrave is like the main house at Castle Dykes (North Stainley) in having a bath-suite in the house as well as the separate baths (Fig. 22, B and Fig. 25,C), Dalton Parlours did not have an internal suite. In many instances in Roman Britain the presence of internal bath-suites and separate large baths suggests that villa owners were providing for the needs of estate workers and their families, even though the expense

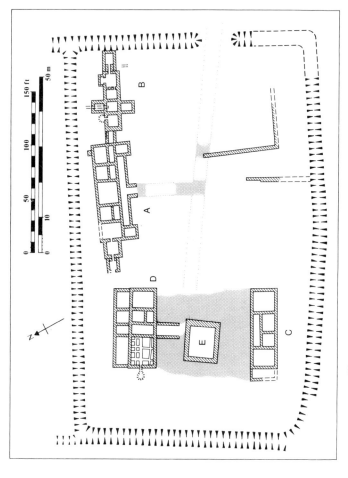

Fig.22. The Gargrave villa in the late third century.

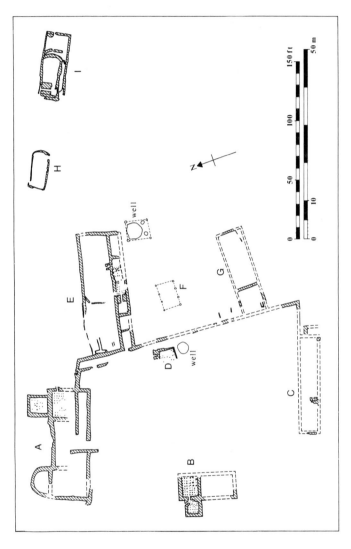

Fig. 23. The Dalton Parlours villa.

Fig.24.   The Dalton Parlours apse mosaic.

of building and maintaining such establishments would
have been considerable. These baths, and even more so, the
large, open-air swimming pool at Well, with its associated
bath buildings, required continuous supplies of water.[19] So
far a water supply using wooden pipes with iron collars has
only been recognized at Gargrave, though Well must
obviously have had one. Dalton Parlours may have relied on
supplies from the two wells found.

Most villas in Britain produce evidence of the addition of
extra domestic accommodation. Sometimes this was done
by expanding the original houses until they eventually
became almost palatial in scale, as at Bignor or North
Leigh.[20] Alternatively, barns were often partly or totally
rebuilt to give additional living quarters in separate
buildings, as at Winterton.[21] Rather more rarely new
purpose-built houses were added, as at Gayton Thorpe.[22]
Our Brigantian villas on the whole seem to avoid elaboration of the original homes, but both at Gargrave and
probably at Castle Dykes (Fig. 25,B) new houses were
added.[23] The additional pair at Gargrave (Fig. 22,C and D).

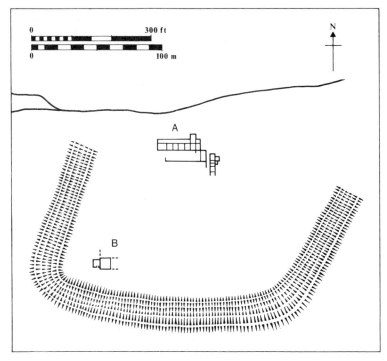

Fig.25. Sketch plan of the Castledykes villa, conflating 19th-century publications.

are contemporary and almost identical, having only four rooms and a corridor each, though both had at least one mosaic floor, the northern one alone having sufficient fragments to say that it belonged to the same type as the unfigured Aldborough ones. For a reconstruction of the likely appearance of the site at this stage see Fig. 26. At Dalton Parlours, a bath-suite (or less probably, heated living rooms) was inserted in a former barn (Fig. 23,B).[24] At Beadlam it looks very much as if the north building began life as a barn, with a wide entrance suitable for carts, later having domestic rooms added, including a hypocaust with a mosaic similar to the one at Gargrave noted above.[25] At Dalton Parlours there were also other buildings in the vicinity of the main house which may have been domestic, but because of the heavy ploughing of the site it will

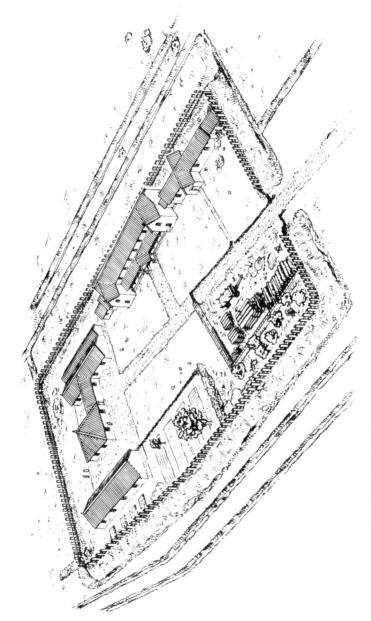

Fig.26. Imaginative reconstruction of the Gargrave villa in the later third century.

probably not be possible to date them. Our villas, then, seem to show similar expansions of populations to ones elsewhere in Britain during the third and, or, fourth centuries. That the extra accommodation was not simply for farm labourers is clear from the nature of the additions. It could perhaps be explained on some sites as quarters for a bailiff who acted as estate manager, particularly in the absence of the owner. This could be true of the additional north house at Gargrave where a single-roomed, squarish building (twice replaced) was at one stage linked to the house by a covered walk (Fig. 22,E). Such square buildings are not uncommon at villas both in Britain and on the Continent. Frequent occurrence of painted wall plaster and tesselated floors in them show that they are not functional farm buildings. They never seem to produce evidence of religious cults and the best interpretation is that they served as the farm offices, where bailiff or owner would issue orders, receive tenants and their rents, and keep the estate records.[26] Alternatively, extra accommodation for owner's sons and their families or the equivalent of dower houses may sometimes have been in question with these additions. The suggestion that villa estates may have been subject to dual or multiple ownership which was reflected in the accommodation does not gain obvious support from the Brigantian evidence.[27]

When we attempt to assess the economic aspect of the Brigantian villa estates, we run into the immediate difficulty that only three sites have functional farm buildings surviving, and at Beadlam little is known about the presumed barn (p. 79). The position of Drax, on land which easily flooded, close to the old course of the Aire, suggests that stock, except perhaps for sheep, would not be raised. Gargrave has produced fragments of three second-century timber-framed buildings with floors of clay and irregular pieces of thin sandstone. One of these had a bill-hook blade trodden into its floor. It was observed that two of the buildings were on the same alignment as the first romanized house and were presumably contemporary with it. As has been noted before, one of the earlier round houses survived into the villa period, since the packing of its final central post was done with hypocaust box-tiles. It was perhaps used as a shelter for labourers in bad weather, or by the builders of the main house. Unfortunately when the nucleus of the site was enclosed (in the early third century?) farm buildings seem to have been excluded from the enclosure, and it was only in the late third century that a partly-walled enclosure, perhaps a stackyard, was inserted in the south-east corner. Presumably other farm buildings lie between the inner and outer enclosures (Fig. 27). Since such structures as we have for Gargrave are not particularly revealing, recourse has to be had to the associated field systems whose ditches partly survive as a surface feature, though not easily understood without the advantage of an aerial view (Fig. 28). Basically, apart from the ditches enclosing the buildings, there are two sets of fields, one very long and narrow, the other a series of more-or-less squared plots perhaps used as paddocks. Unfortunately, mediaeval and later systems overlie the Roman fields to the south of the site, while modern ploughing has removed most of the evidence to the west. However, it is clear that the fields were bounded by the Aire on the north and by a beck to the south. The probable minimum area of the fields is of the order of 40 ha (100 acres), but that of course does not allow for the possibility of adjacent sheep and cattle grazing on unenclosed moorland. The forms of the fields seem to suggest a mixture of ploughland using the heavy plough on narrow fields and of corralling of stock (paddock-like fields). Unfortunately, the soil is so acid that animal bones rarely survive and only the pig is firmly attested by several finds, implying some uncleared woodland. We have already mentioned that a piped water supply was laid into the baths, but it will also have been used to supply water for stock. The aerial photographs clearly show a rectangular hollow just inside the eastern boundary of the main enclosure, and since the aqueduct will have entered the site on that side, it seems highly likely that this was the main reservoir. Alternatively, it could have been a fish pond.

Mentioning woodland in connexion with pigs serves as a reminder that on Roman estates there must always have been major reserves of timber. Quite apart from its use in

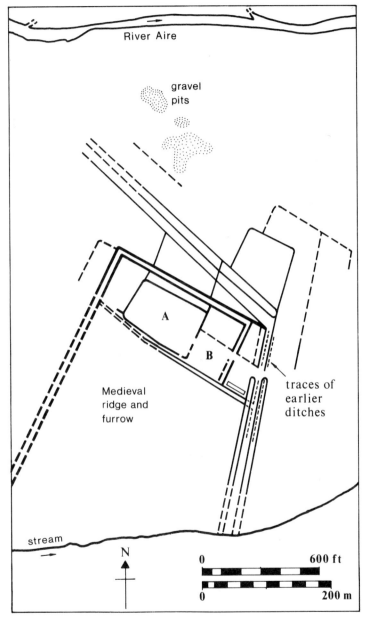

Fig.27. The surviving evidence for the fields of the Gargrave villa.

Fig.28.   The Gargrave field system from the air.

initial construction and repair of buildings, it was needed
extensively for farm equipment and in transport. But above
all, it served as virtually the only source of fuel, sometimes
in the form of charcoal. The bathhouse and other hypocausts at Gargrave would have needed tens of acres of
woodland available for coppicing.[28] Similarly in initial
construction of the villa building, fuel was needed to serve
lime-kilns which will have existed on the estate, as well as
the kiln suggested by the peculiar local forms of tile used.
No doubt the estate blacksmith also produced the iron nails
and other objects needed for construction as well as making
and maintaining farm equipment. It is appropriate that
Gargrave has produced a billhook.

For Dalton Parlours the available evidence seems to point
to considerable cereal production in view of the T-shaped
furnaces usually thought to be for drying corn, but perhaps
really malting ovens for beer production.[29] The quern
emplacements in some of the lesser sunken buildings also

point to cereal crops.[30] It is not clear how far the Iron Age ditch system remained in use during the Roman period, though evidently some of it did, as ditches surrounding apparent Iron Age features have painted wall plaster in their fillings.[31] The farming buildings at the villa were carefully separated from the domestic part as at Gargrave, but this time by a dividing wall (Fig. 23). Two large barn-like buildings existed in the eastern half, one containing T-shaped kilns and having inserted (?) heated rooms along the south side. The other was poorly preserved but evidently had one heated room, not necessarily domestic. The most curious functional buildings, however, were four structures with semi-basements, some containing quern emplacements and at least one with another T-shaped furnace. There were also two similar but much smaller buildings. These sunken structures are without parallel in our area, but presumably the nature of the subsoil, which is well drained, made it possible to use them.

In summary it will be seen that the Brigantian villas never reach the most elaborate levels of development found elsewhere in Britain, but that it would be misleading to judge them from the main villa houses. Their bathhouses can be as impressive as any elsewhere, and their mosaic floors are often of tolerable quality. The presence of such sites on the east side of the Pennines where they are more or less closely related to Brigantian towns and *vici* only serves to point out the contrast between the east and west side of the Pennines once more.

Rural Shrines

One final aspect of rural life in Brigantia calls for mention, namely religious activity. Only one site with structural remains of shrines is known to us, the one on Scargill Moor, near Bowes, where army officers dedicated altars to the otherwise unknown Vinotonus who was equated on one with Silvanus. He must have been a god of the wild, and presumably patron of hunters.[32] That many similar shrines will once have existed is suggested by finds of altars like the famous one from Weardale dedicated by the commander of the *ala Sebosiana*, boasting that he has bagged a splendid boar which many others had failed to get (*RIB* 1041). Once more the altar is to Silvanus, but this time a previous dedication to the imperial cult was erased.[33] This must have been brought from a fort or its *vicus*. The prefect was evidently a bold man, as he not only dealt with the boar but added sacrilege to his exploits.

Other rural cults are also attested by altars, such as some of those to Dea Brigantia, or the one to Apollo at Scarcroft which may have had an associated shrine.[34] Major temples and pilgrimage centres are so far conspicuously lacking in the countryside of Brigantia, where religious observance was evidently much more a domestic and private matter, when not associated with cults practised in the towns and *vici*.

5

Industry and the Economy

Brigantia was no exception to the general rule that the basis of wealth in the Roman world rested on the ownership of land and on the products of it, whether vegetable or animal. As we have seen, the general emphasis in northern Britain was on pastoralism rather than agriculture. While it is now much more widely accepted than formerly that cereal crops were grown fairly extensively in the north, it is perhaps unlikely that such produce was exported from the area. On the other hand, animals and products from them will certainly have formed the major items of trade going out of Brigantia. Nevertheless, it is clear that exploitation of other resources such as minerals, stone and clay will have added appreciably to the basic farming economy. As in all areas on the fringes of the Roman empire, the presence of the army clearly served as a major stimulus to local enterprise, a presence also attractive to traders from other parts of the Roman world. Much of Brigantia has evidence of mining and industrial activity (Fig. 29).

Mining

There is no doubt that mining experts would have explored the Pennine area as soon as the army took over in Agricola's governorship, and it is striking that lead was already being worked in Nidderdale by A.D.81, and also in Derbyshire in the Flavian period, if the name cast on Derbyshire pigs in the form TI.CL.TR. is to be identified with the one struck cold on Vespasianic pigs from the Mendips in the form TI.CL.TRIF.[1] There may, however, have been initial dis-

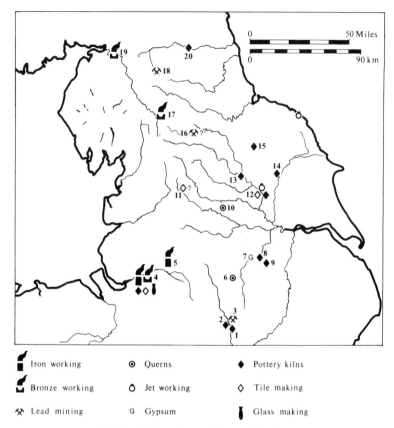

Fig.29.   Brigantian mining and industry.

appointment with the mineral resources, since no gold was
found, and some of the lead ores, notably those of
Derbyshire, had very low silver content.[2] If this is correct,
then it becomes clear that the two areas were worked
differently, since the Yorkshire pigs have imperial names
cast on them, ranging from Domitian to Hadrian, whereas
in Derbyshire the name TI.CL.TR. was cast and implies
leasing of mining concessions to private exploiters. This
tradition for Derbyshire is confirmed by the appearance of
other private names and more interestingly the mention of a
socio (company) associated with Lutudarum, assumed to be
in the Matlock area (Fig. 29,3).[3] Perhaps one reason for the

leasing of concessions by the procurator was the low silver content of the Derbyshire ores. But it seems that the concessions may have been withdrawn at least for a time under Hadrian, for a pig specifically tied to Lutadarum has his name cast on it.[4] As long as working was done directly by the government, no profit accrued to the area. Once a local company or individual concessionaires were involved, some of the profits would be in circulation in the area. The presence of at least six pigs at Brough-on-Humber suggests that it served as a point of export for the Derbyshire mines.

It has also been argued that the Alston lead mines (Fig. 29,18) were worked in the Roman period, but that rests largely upon the presence of a lead sealing at Brough-under-Stainmore with the stamp of Cohors II Nerviorum, which has METAL(LVM) on the reverse. The interpretation is less than certain, and several of the other sealings have abbreviated personal names in this position. There is, however, galena recorded from the fort at Whitley Castle, where the cohort was stationed in the third century.[5] If the interpretation of the sealing is right, the activity involved could equally have been the mining of copper ores, which are also to be found at Alston. In view of the eight or more army units with seals at Brough, it is evident that material was being sent there from many places. Failing Alston as a source, there is no evidence for the exploitation of copper ores within Brigantia. Nevertheless, industries based on copper alloys were present, for instance at Brough itself and at Stanwix.[6]

There is no lack of iron ore in Brigantia and presumably most deposits were worked during the Roman period, though there are now no surviving traces of the methods, probably always opencast, used to win the raw material. Clear evidence for iron working in their vicinities suggest that the Cleveland, Durham, Northumbrian and Cumbrian sources were all exploited. The evidence for the use of the West Riding ores is less compelling.

In the smelting of the metallic ores it was, of course, essential to have fuels and reducing agents. These were normally combined in the form of coal or charcoal mixed with the ores. The production of charcoal will have gone on everywhere in wooded areas, and there is evidence that several of the main coal outcrops were worked in the Roman period including the Northumberland-Durham fields, outcrops in the Leeds area, and parts of the Lancashire coal fields. Some of the coal seems to have been exported to the south of Britain.[7] It was used in metal-working particularly. In discussing metal-working in the area it is necessary to try to distinguish between smelting of the ores and the manufacturing of objects. In general in Roman Britain smelting tends to be confined to specialist settlements or to small-scale working in rural areas. The production and finishing of metal objects was something which, like blacksmithing until recent times, was carried on everywhere. Of specialist sites we can point to the *vicus* of the fort at Manchester with its large assemblage of over thirty smelting and smithing furnaces (Fig. 29,5). It also has a probable example of a furnace for hardening iron by the process of carburization, that is by adding carbon to the white-hot metal to convert cutting edges and the like into a steel.[8] Another site which we can consider probably Brigantian, although it could conceivably have been Cornovian, is that at Wilderspool on the south bank of the Mersey, at the meeting point of the roads from Middlewich and Chester (Fig. 29,4). The settlement there was involved in several kinds of industrial activity including smelting, metal-working, possibly the manufacture of glass, and it was also a major pottery. Although many of the details of the metal-working remain obscure, recent reappraisal of Thomas May's records makes it clear that the smelting of iron and the production of objects in both iron and bronze was involved.[9] An unusual furnace designed to heat crucibles during the process of making bronze alloys has been firmly identified, and one of the crucibles found was encrusted with a bronze containing some zinc in addition to the basic copper and tin, thus suggesting that it was a wrought bronze that was to be made.[10] Whether enamelling of bronzes was also carried out here, as Thomas May thought, is perhaps less certain, though enamelled brooches were relatively common at the site and the northern tradition of enamelling current in the Iron Age was continued, as the northern trumpet brooches show.[11] The enamelled souvenir bowls portraying Hadrian's Wall also are surely more likely to be northern rather than southern products.[12] For the most part, however, the evidence for the manufacture of metal objects is on a small scale and comes both from the towns and the *vici* of forts. Smithing will have been ubiquitous, but the finishing of bronzes is attested at York and Catterick and the former may have been involved in casting, in view of a crucible found in the same workshop.[13] Examples of bronze-working in the *vici* occur at Brough-under-Stainmore and Stanwix, both producing flawed castings of a wide variety of objects including a second-century trumpet brooch characteristic of the north.[14] Of working in the precious metals, there is little direct evidence. The raw materials would almost certainly have to be imported into the area, but of the existence of workers in these materials we may be reasonably certain. The gold brooch from Aesica, for instance, is no doubt a northern product and probably of the late first century. The silver brooch found with it in the same hoard also betrays the hand of a northern craftsman, though probably one working some 50 or 60 years later.[15] There is one intriguing object from the line of Hadrian's Wall near Halton Chesters which must be connected with the production of gold jewellery. It is a shale plaque with engraved designs clearly intended for producing gold orna- ments made from foil with a backing of composition. The designs for the most part are simple roundels or *peltae*, but there are also a couple of human heads, neither particularly Celtic in style, and the mould may well have belonged to an immigrant craftsman (Fig. 30).[16]

Just as the Aesica brooch shows strong native influence in its decoration, so too do some of the bronzes of the north. It is quite clear, as might be expected from the strong Iron Age tradition of decorative metalwork, that manufacture of objects in native taste continued far into the Roman period, gradually being swamped by the more banal Roman types during the course of the second century. Good examples of this are the bronze mountings from cauldrons, buckets and the like from such places as Kirkby Lonsdale and Manches- ter, or the remarkable head from Aldborough (Fig. 4).[17] The demand for bronzes of all kinds must have grown enor-

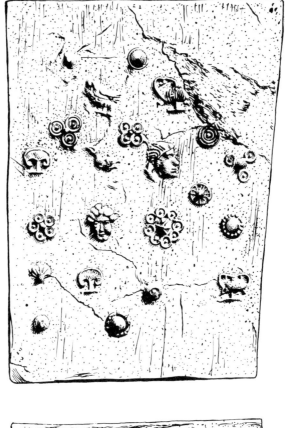

Fig.30. Drawing from the cast of a shale plaque (now lost) found near Halton Chesters (¼).

mously during the Roman period, and presumably native suppliers are likely to have been responsible for producing at least some of the material used by troops, on the analogy of practice elsewhere in the Empire.

Civilian smelting and smithing of iron on the large scale is so far only attested for Wilderspool and Manchester, but more large centres and many local ones will undoubtedly have been needed to supply the total demands of the area. However, much of the archaeological evidence for such activity is suspect since the 'slag' so often recorded in excavation has rarely been examined scientifically and a good deal of it is probably no more than clinker from furnaces which might have had a multitude of purposes.

Lead turns up on all romanized sites and on many at a relatively low level of romanization. It was no doubt used in building in the form of flashing for roofs, but lead pipes for supplying water were not in general use; lead waste pipes draining plunge baths were relatively more common. Some lead found its way into bronzes, particularly where casting was needed, but more will have been used in the cinerary *ossuaria* of the earlier, and coffins of the later, Roman period. As noted above (p. 56) York has a notable series of lead coffins, mostly undecorated. Otherwise the only major object attested in the north is a large lead vat from Ireby in Cumbria of the kind often carrying *chi-rho* monograms and undoubtedly connected with Christian ritual.[18] Since the melting of lead requires only a low temperature and its casting and fashioning is relatively simple, we should expect production to have been carried on at the local level for the most part. Of the major metal-working sites, Wilderspool alone has produced possible evidence for working in lead. There is no evidence for northern production of pewter, apart from the mould from the Langton Villa, probably used for producing pewter dishes, and pewter is noticeably rare in Brigantia.[19]

Stone

If we think in terms of the sheer bulk of material, then the industries centred around the exploitation of stone must have been among the largest in the north. Many civilian sites went through an initial stage of timber buildings, but almost everywhere in the second century building in masonry was common at romanized sites. Quarries supplying local needs will have appeared over the whole of Brigantia. Some indeed may have followed on the workings needed to provide road foundations and metalling in the later first century. Since the Pennines form the backbone of the area, it is scarcely surprising that Millstone Grit was very widely used, particularly when large blocks were required. But the Pennines in fact have a great range of stones including much limestone and some finer grits, and sandstones. These two were used locally but rarely seem to have been carried to neighbouring areas, though the Millstone Grit regularly was, as its presence at sites like Aldborough, Catterick and York shows. In adjacent areas much use was made of the more local limestones and sandstones, as at York where Magnesian Limestone from Tadcaster was very prominent, or at Aldborough where the

Fig.31. The Wolf and Twins pavement from Aldborough.

local red sandstone seems to have been more important than the Millstone Grit.

Similarly on the west side of the Pennines, the sandstones of Lancashire and the Eden Valley were much in demand. That a Brigantian firm of mosaicists was active in the third century, whether at York or Aldborough, is attested by the similarities of designs at the two towns, and the presence of mosaics which belong to the same class at Gargrave, Beadlam and Hovingham. Although there are some links with Smith's Petuarian School, the differences are also considerable but, more important, the Brigantian mosaics begin earlier. Aldborough's peculiar mosaic of the Wolf and Twins, if genuine, is clearly later than most of the mosaics there, and Smith considers it a product of the Petuarian School (Fig. 31).[20]

One point that needs stressing is that on the whole in northern Britain buildings tended to be carried up in stone to their full heights, thus increasing the demand for dressed stone but also requiring considerable quantities of lime mortar, so that the industry of lime-burning will always have been considerable even if evidence of civilian kilns is totally wanting. So, too, the digging and transport of sand, and to a lesser degree gravel, will have been constant. That masons, skilled enough to produce such embellishments as turned columns and bases, were available by the later second century is clear from the evidence at many sites. But one looks in vain for the more refined versions of Graeco-Roman architecture, and the general impression given by both architectural fragments and by stones with reliefs is of a considerable degree of rusticity. There are few notable exceptions, the most striking being the sandstone tomb-stones of Regina and Victor at South Shields.[21] In the more intractable gritstone, a few of the York *sarcophagi* are by no means incompetently decorated (Fig. 32). They will serve, too, as a reminder that, particularly in the later Roman period, there was a demand on the part of the wealthy inhabitants of York for such weighty, and no doubt costly, items, which were placed in *mausolea* as their decoration shows.

The quarrying and dressing of gritstone for use as dom-

Fig.32.   Sarcophagus of Iulia Victorina.

estic querns will always have been a major preoccupation in
the Pennines themselves. A factory at Wharncliffe, near
Sheffield (Fig. 29,6), produced romanized flat querns at the
same time as the traditional beehive ones,[22] and Adel near
Leeds is believed to have produced unfinished querns (Fig.
29,10). But such activity will have been much more widespread,
and export of the querns from Brigantia is not doubted. Large
millstones for use in powered mills were probably confined to
use by the army and will have been made by it.[23]

There remain some specialized stone industries, namely
the use of jet from the Jurassic outcrops on the northeast
Yorkshire coast, and gypsum from the Tadcaster area. Some
jet objects were produced locally, though the sites are more
at the homestead level than anything else and major export
of finished objects from the Whitby area seems unlikely.
Much more promising as the source of the manufactured
objects found all over Britain, and occasionally in the
Rhineland, is the factory known to have existed on the
fringes of the town at York, discovered under the existing

Railway Station and succeeded in the later Roman period by a cemetery. The craftsmen at York produced, alongside the usual carved pins, beads and bangles, some extraordinarily finely-carved pins with thistle-like heads and a remarkable series of pendant amulets, some of them family groups, some apparently betrothal pieces, and others with conventional masks including gorgon heads (Fig. 33). Nor should one forget the charming little jet bears which no doubt delighted the small children for whom they were intended.[24] While more jet objects tend to be found in the North than elsewhere, they are by no means lacking in the Midlands and South. Perhaps both finished objects and unworked jet left Brigantia, since there is a suspicion of manufacture of

Fig.33. Jet objects from York (¾).

objects at Leicester, for instance.[25] The jet objects from the Rhineland are usually accepted as exports from Brigantia and so particularly interesting as trade in finished products.[26] As for the gypsum, that must have been used in wall-plastering and mouldings, but we know it best from the remarkable series of inhumations, particularly from York, in which liquid gypsum was poured into the coffin, presumably in an attempt to preserve the bodies it encased. This rite is not confined to York, nor even to Brigantia, but it does seem to have been particularly popular in and around the Vale of York, no doubt because of the local sources of gypsum. Such burials are often held to be specifically Christian (p. 56).

Clay

There was no lack of clay suitable for making tiles and pottery in Brigantia, but thin-bedded stone was common, so roofing was often of stone slabs, and there is no certain civilian tile-kiln known. Although army units, both legionary and auxiliary, certainly made their own tiles, as at York, Grimescar, Quernmore near Lancaster or Muncaster near Ravenglass, even they tended more often to use stone slabs as roofing. It should be remembered, however, that bath-suites almost inevitably required tiles for hypocaust systems, and it is unlikely that they came from distant sources. The existence of some civilian kilns may be inferred from indirect evidence. For instance, the town at York has produced a series of antefixes mostly with extraordinarily crude decoration.[27] No doubt civilian tilers were imitating the legion in using antefixes at all. Interestingly enough, it seems that York could boast a *collegium* which concerned itself, in part at least, with craftsmen producing tiles, since a *graffito* incised before firing and reading POLIO/COLEGIO/FELICTER (Fig. 34) was found in the 18th century in Montague Gile's brickyard in Clifton, well outside the fortress.[28] Another example of what must have been local production, though perhaps on the estate itself, is given by the large series of roofing and hypocaust tiles from the villa

Fig.34. Tile (now lost) from Clifton, York with inscription wishing a guild (presumably of tile-makers) good fortune.

at Gargrave (Fig. 29,11). Most of them, although approximating to standard Roman forms, betray local idiosyncrasies. Finally, what may have been tile kilns are reported from Wilderspool, associated with apparent wasters (Fig. 29,4).[29]

Turning to pottery, the first and obvious point to be made is that there was no strong pre-Roman tradition in Brigantia. The crude, ill-fired, handmade pottery found on some Iron Age sites must have been made at domestic level. Already before the annexation by Rome, a demand for romanized pottery was beginning to make itself felt, as the evidence from Stanwick shows. With the arrival of the Roman army in our area, civilian demand for Roman pottery will obviously have increased considerably. At the same time, the army units themselves seem initially to have been drawing largely on supplies from military kilns, though they were not above making occasional use of local handmade wares. Even when army production declined in the Hadrianic period, suppliers of pottery tended to be in the Midlands and south of Britain rather than the north. Indeed, until the fourth century, all of the really major potteries fell to the south of Brigantia. Nevertheless, the desire of some southern potters to capture northern markets led to migration into our area. It is not always easy to pin this down as precisely as is possible for Rossington Bridge, near Doncaster (Fig. 29,9), where in the Antonine period one of the major mortarium makers of the Midlands, Sarrius of Mancetter, seems to have established a branch of his firm run by a man named Setibogius.[30] Their mortaria then travelled as far north as the Antonine Wall. We might visualize a similar process at work at Wilderspool slightly earlier in the second century, since the affinities of the vessels produced suggest the probability of potters from the West Midlands moving to the site. The mortaria produced there have a wide distribution along the west side of the Pennines, are common on, and in the vicinity of, Hadrian's Wall, but also reached the Antonine Wall. The pattern may have been repeated later, if the potter Austinus began work at Wilderspool, since it seems likely that he later operated further north, perhaps in the Eden Valley area.[31]

It is now known that civilian production at York had been established before the middle of the second century, as mortaria with stamps of local potters have turned up at recently-located kilns at Heworth. The fabrics are similar to those used earlier by the legionary potters.[32] Other coarse pottery from York, in much the same fabric as the probable legionary products, was current in the later second century, when legionary kilns were unlikely to have been at work. The most likely explanation is that veterans of the York legion, trained in the manufacture of pottery, established their own kilns on discharge from the army, and that they and their successors continued producing in much the same tradition.[33]

It has been thought that an attempt to produce moulded samian ware may have been made at York. The evidence is equivocal and consists solely of the presence of two pieces of moulds for making bowls of form 37. The larger is from a mould of Drusus i who worked at Les Martres-de-Veyre, near Clermont-Ferrand, early in the second century. The other fragment is too small for its source to be identified. These fragments are known to have come from the industrial area under the present Railway Station.[34] Even if they were imported in antiquity, as is possible, their presence does not necessarily give evidence for an attempt to produce true samian ware, since they could have been used to turn out bowls in coarse ware. Needless to say, there are no examples either of samian or of coarse ware imitations known in our area which could be even remotely connected with them.

To return to Rossington Bridge, it is worth noting that in addition to mortaria, close imitations of black-burnished ware, category 1, were also being made by the middle of the second century.[35] This production may also have been initiated by a potter or potters from the south, since at least one example of a straight-sided dish with applied vertical bars, otherwise confined to the Durotrigian area, the homeland of black-burnished ware, has also been found at the kilns, and there are close similarities in the forms produced. Unfortunately, apart from the stamped mortaria, it is very difficult to pin down the distribution of the pottery from Rossington and from other kilns in the neighbourhood, notably those at Cantley (Fig. 28,8). Probably they were mainly concerned with supplying the large number of native sites in south-western Yorkshire, as well as Doncaster itself.

Other potteries active in the second century almost certainly included one at Aldborough (Fig. 29,13) where mortaria, and no doubt other classes of vessels, were produced and Corbridge (Fig. 29,20), which has yielded a die for stamping mortaria.[36] Indeed, there were probably several potteries working at a moderate scale in the northeast, if one may judge from the stamped mortaria with relatively localized distributions in a variety of fabrics. At Corbridge, jars with characteristic appliqué decoration including deities were locally made.[37] Later production in the Brigantian area is singularly poorly attested. One class of ware which might be mentioned is the series of hard-grey, wheel-turned jars, based on black-burnished ware types, which was current in the Vale of York and the Yorkshire Pennines in the late second and early third centuries. However, their precise source is unknown. Some coarse, gritty handmade pots with similar distribution seem to have been made at the Cold Cam Kiln, Cockerdale, though possibly elsewhere, too.[38] Two other classes of coarse pottery merit mention, namely Derbyshire ware and Dales ware. The former, originally with a restricted distribution in and around Derbyshire in the second century, became much more widely distributed in the north in the late third and early fourth centuries. Some of the kilns producing it are known from Holbrook and Hazelwood (Fig. 29,1,2).[39] Similarly, jars of Dales ware type seem to have been current in the southern fringes of our area long before they became common over much of it in the second half of the third century in standardized shell-gritted fabric. Their source is not known but is likely to have been on the east side of the Pennines probably, but not certainly, within Brigantia. Local imitations of the basic type seem to have been produced near York. Despite this and similar evidence for production of pottery within Brigantia in the second and third centuries, it remains clear that the bulk of pottery used in our area continued to be imported from abroad or from further south. This remained true even when samian ware ceased to be imported, since British colour-coated ware, almost all from further south, must have replaced it on the table. Changes during the course of the fourth century only serve to emphasize the dependence of the *civitas* on external sources, as the pots of the later fourth century which swamped our area came almost entirely from kilns in the territory of the Parisi, at such centres as Crambeck or, for some of the finer wares, from the Nene Valley.

For the many other potential industrial activities, evidence is largely lacking, but it may just be worth considering briefly the production of glass. There can be little doubt that window glass will have been produced at many of the larger sites, but there has always been a curious reluctance to accept the possibility that glass tableware was produced in Britain. Recent evidence from sites outside Brigantia combines to make the chances of such manufacture seem higher. While the evidence from Wilderspool is by no means conclusive, it does seem quite possible that glass was made there, and the local presence of sands suitable for glass-making adds some support for the idea.[40] It would not be surprising if in the future evidence appears from other northern sites, and indeed one might suggest York as a potential candidate in view of some sets of vessels clearly all from the same workshop.

Products of the Land and Sea

As has been observed above, the production of cereal crops was by no means neglected in suitable terrain within Brigantia. We have no figures, needless to say, on which to assess this, but it would be surprising indeed if any surplus remained once the needs of the army and the inhabitants of the *civitas* itself had been satisfied. Indeed, one might expect some importation of cereals into the area. For the lesser crops our evidence is virtually silent and speculation is pointless. We must, however, remind ourselves of the importance of wood as a crop. We have already seen good reasons why villa estates had a high proportion of woodland.[41] Towns will obviously have needed considerable areas of woodland to draw on, and it is unlikely that villa estates supplied all their needs. And here it should be remembered that seasoned timber would be desirable for some purposes and essential for others, so that timber merchants will eventually have had bases in or near the towns.

When we turn to stock-raising, however, although we cannot begin to quantify production, it is obviously likely that the inevitable emphasis on sheep and cattle in the multitude of farmsteads in the hill areas will have led to a net surplus. Export of animals to other areas is perhaps unlikely, but the export of their products, particularly wool and hides, must be invoked to explain the large quantities of imported goods everywhere available. That said, one is bound to admit that there is no direct evidence for export. However, merchants trading with Britain and entering such rivers as the Ouse and the Tyne will scarcely have been content to depart merely in ballast, and it is difficult to see what they would be carrying in bulk other than wool, hides or occasionally animals for use in the arena or in hunting.

Of the production of textiles or the preparation of leather we have no evidence at all from Brigantia, unless we can accept the evidence suggested for domestic spinning and weaving provided by the so-called carding-combs and spindle whorls (both classes of objects having other potential uses).[42] One negative piece of evidence is striking, namely the extreme rarity of loom weights in Roman domestic contexts. Several explanations come to mind: one being that the bulk of the wool was sent elsewhere for treatment, another that there was some degree of concentration of processing at a few large establishments. Alternatively, it could be conjectured that warp-weighted looms were not used.

When it comes to linen, we have even less evidence. The presence of linen cloth in graves at York is not sound evidence for local production, however attractive the idea might be, in view of its later prominence in the Knaresborough area, for instance. Since we know virtually nothing of the Roman horizons in the floor of the Vale of York, conjecture about it as a possible source of flax is best left aside. Similarly, apart from the military depot at Catterick, Brigantia has produced no evidence of tanneries, though obviously local production of leather goods will have gone on in or near every settlement of any size.

An occupation which leaves little trace in the archaeological record is that of fishing which, remembering the long coastlines of Brigantia, must have been of major importance. Indeed, one aspect of it does obtrude regularly in the form of oyster and mussel shells found on all sites, no matter how far inland. Transport of shellfish in containers with their native water will have been the only practical method of distribution.[43] Ordinary fish caught off the coasts would have to be smoked or salted if they were to be transported over long distances. Evidence is entirely wanting. But that the rivers would have been fished, no doubt strenuously in the vicinity of large settlements, there is no reason to question, and a remarkable antefix from York, unhappily not complete, shows a fisherman with net and trap (Fig. 35).[44] York also may have evidence of preparation of fish on a large scale (for sauce?) in the late fourth century.[45] Until very recently our rivers have been so polluted that we tend to forget the commercial importance of inland fishing, but its value in former times was considerable.[46] The need to salt fish for long-range transport is a reminder of the importance of salt in other aspects of the economy, since demand for it would be inevitable and

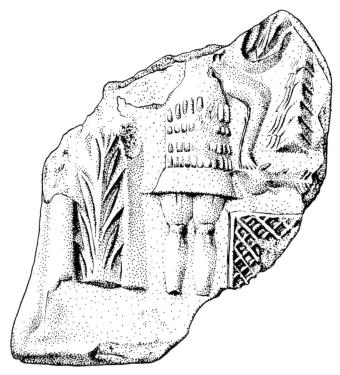

Fig.35. Eaves tile *(antefix)* from York, showing a fisherman with stylised trap and net holding part of his catch (½).

constant. Erosion along the northeast coast is likely to have removed evidence of any salterns that may have existed, though attention ought to be paid to some of the major estuaries with this point in mind.

Commerce

If we now think of the balance of trade within our areas, it will soon become apparent that during the earlier Roman period the quantities of imported commodities will have been immense. We have only to name such things as the trade in samian ware at first from South Gaul, and then during the second century, from Central Gaulish factories, and finally from sources in the Rhineland and Moselle in the later second and earlier third century. The quantities imported at this last stage were, however, much reduced, though the so-called Rhenish ware and some large mortaria also came from those areas. Similarly, the importation of Spanish *amphorae* as containers primarily of oil and fish-sauce (*garum*) came to an end at the beginning of the third century.[47] By this time our area must have been self-sufficient in many categories of manufactured goods, and probably only the finer varieties of glass and metal table-ware had to be imported. Set against that, the effect of the *pax Romana* and the development of farming should have given larger surpluses of primary materials for export. Nor would loans from Italian financiers have been needed by communities within the *civitas* in this period. The result of the various changes probably meant a much healthier economic state, and even the demands of the army had probably decreased during the course of the third century.

Of the merchants engaged in trading, whether internal or external, we naturally have our best evidence in the form of inscriptions from York and from the vicinity of the northern frontier. Corbridge has produced the well-known tombstone of Barates the Palmyrene, who evidently made a living by selling flags to the army. He clearly prospered, since he could afford a particularly fine tombstone for Regina, a Catuvellaunian girl whom he had bought as a slave and subsequently freed and married. She died at the age of 30, and was buried at South Shields. The cosmopolitan nature of the frontier settlements is underlined by another tomb-stone from South Shields dedicated to a Moor who was the freedman of an auxiliary trooper.[48] He was presumably engaged in commercial activity on behalf of his former owner. Although we do not know his origin, the Antonianus who promised to gild an inscription at Bowness if his venture was successful, is likely also to have been a merchant.[49]

York has recently produced a fragmentary inscription of unusual interest, since it can be firmly linked with another found off the mouth of the Rhine at Colijnsplaat, where Placidus, son of Viducus, describes himself as *negotiator*

Britannicianus, along with many others who use the same
description, some of whom will have been trading with the
north of Britain (Fig. 36). At York Placidus has become a
Roman citizen and uses his father's name modified as his
nomen; his new style is L. Viducius [Viduci f(ilius)] Placidus,
and he firmly associates himself with the tribe of the
Veliocasses centred on Rouen.[50] It thus seems that Placidus
is likely to have been involved in trade between his home
area and the Rhineland, as well as between the Rhineland
and Britain. He, and some of his fellows, could well have
been among the *negotiatores cretariae* involved in the shipping
of the Rhenish and Moselle pottery mentioned above. He
was evidently successful in at least one of his enterprises,
since he was able to embellish a temple at York with an arch
and another architectural feature. Another Gaul at York
was M. Verecundius Diogenes who was a *sevir Augustalis* of
the *colonia* and a Biturix Cubus from the Bourges area. He

Fig.36.   Fragmentary inscription of L. Viducius Placidus (p. 106)

was, incidentally, married to a Sardinian.[51] Holding the sevirate and with such a *cognomen*, he can scarcely have been anything but a freedman. It is virtually certain that he will have been engaged in commerce, and indeed on one restoration of the somewhat corrupt text for his *sarcophagus*, last seen being used as a horse trough in Hull, he is taken to be a *moritex* (shipper?).[52] There may be slight doubt about Diogenes, but there can scarcely be any about M. Aurelius Lunaris.[53] He held the sevirate in both Lincoln and York, and his *cognomen* is again suspiciously servile. When he sailed from York in A.D.237, he evidently vowed to set up an altar if he arrived safely at his destination, Bordeaux. He took the precaution of carrying a large block of Millstone Grit with him and eventually dedicated it *De(ae) Tutel[a]e Boudig(ae)*. The latter is often taken to be the name of a goddess, homonymous with the better known Boudica. But this is surely a blunder for the *tutela* of B(o)urdigala (Bordeaux). However, although the stone is slightly damaged, there is no question of the 'R' ever having been present. Lunaris can scarcely have been a wine merchant and nothing else, since even if he were importing wine to Britain, he must have been exporting something else from Britain. In fact, there is no evidence at all that he was connected with the wine trade, although oil, or resin, are perhaps the only other likely exports from Bordeaux at that period.

The inscriptions may be few in number, but they are extremely revealing, and it is interesting that not one of them shows a native Briton involved in commerce. They serve again as a reminder that towns like York or civil settlements outside forts like South Shields had an exceedingly mixed population in the Roman period. It will be observed that direct continental trade into the west coast ports is singularly ill-attested, nor is this surprising. The relatively short, easy landfall from the mouth of the Rhine to the east coast is the controlling factor. Furthermore, there was a major corporation active in that area, the *negotiatores Britanniciani*.[54] No doubt the hazards, real or imagined, of the Irish Sea also had some effect.

6

A.D. 367 and After

A.D.367 is taken as a major divide in the history of Roman
Britain because it was then that for the first time diverse
elements outside the Roman provinces conspired together
to make concerted attacks. Ammianus Marcellinus, often
called the fourth-century Tacitus, is the source of this
belief.[1] In recent years, however, it has been usual to
consider that his picture of Britain in dire straits was
overdrawn. Even in the south, no towns and few villas
(except in the southwest) show destructions which might
coincide with A.D.367.[2] Nor does this period show any
increase in coin hoarding in Britain. Paradoxically, however, evidence for the subsequent restoration of the diocese
by Theodosius, one of Valentinian's *comites rei militaris*, has
been much stressed.[3]

What did or did not happen in Brigantia in A.D.367?
First, there is no evidence that any civilian site, town, *vicus*,
or villa was then destroyed, with the possible exception of
Corbridge.[4] We can indeed go further and say firmly that
many sites definitely were not destroyed. As for Hadrian's
Wall itself, it is clear that there was much rebuilding around
A.D.370, but in recent years previous destruction has only
been claimed for Chesters.[5] Furthermore, when Ammianus
states that *areani* were removed from office because they had
revealed what was going on in the province to the barbarians, he implies that their duties were beyond the Wall
keeping a watch on the tribes in Scotland. He nowhere says
that the frontier was attacked, still less that it was
destroyed.[6] When we turn to the forts south of the Wall, the
evidence for destruction is equally unimpressive. True, the

forts at Bainbridge, Bowes, Ilkley, Malton, and Piercebridge were all rebuilt in the late fourth century, very probably all during a Theodosian restoration. Not one, however, has produced firm evidence of previous destruction rather than decay.[7] The reconstructions which are well-attested both on the Wall and in the hinterland forts never involved modernizing of defences with bastions, and they probably point to necessary work after a period of neglect like that postulated for the later third century (p. 31). It was presumably at this period that levies from southern *civitates* were at work restoring Hadrian's Wall.[8] Nevertheless, new military sites did appear in the late fourth century near Carlisle, namely at Barrock Fell and Wreay Hall.[9] On the Yorkshire coast of Brigantia, and perhaps also the Durham coast, the well-known signal stations with their massive central towers were now built, probably by Theodosius, though a recent study has suggested a later context.[10] These new structures suggest anxiety about their particular vicinities and perhaps imply previous barbarian incursions. That possibility apart, it will be seen that there is virtually no evidence for destruction anywhere in Brigantia in A.D.367. The troubles must have been almost confined to the south. We have seen that southern *civitates* were providing labour for work on the Wall and obviously the Brigantes would also be required to produce similar labour. There is almost certainly epigraphic confirmation.[11]

Despite the lack of destruction in *vici*, it is clear that they were normally abandoned before A.D.370. This has usually been taken as one of the results of the war of 367–9. In fact, *vici* were not necessarily all given up simultaneously, nor need any particular *vicus* have been totally abandoned at one time. The implication may rather be that *vicani* were moving into the forts where, on Hadrian's Wall at least, the 'chalet' type of barracks, looking singularly like separate flats suitable for use as married-quarters, were being built in the restorations usually assigned to Constantius, and, incidentally, occurred beyond the Wall at High Rochester.[12] These buildings were still in use with only minor modifications at Housesteads in the final phase, when civilians were clearly there. The reason usually accepted for the presence of

women and children in the forts in the fourth century is that
the army units on the Wall and, by implication elsewhere,
were now something more like a peasant militia, and
evidently their strengths were far below those of the old-style
cohorts and alas, hence the availability of space in the forts.

The Theodosian restoration in the north was largely a
matter of seeing that Hadrian's Wall functioned as an
effective military obstacle, of seeing that the forts behind it
were renewed, and of dealing with coastal defence. The new
coastal signal stations on the east coast and some existing
establishments on the west coast, such as the massive fort of
Saxon Shore type at Lancaster, the only example of the new
military architecture in the north, were evidently intended
for cooperation with the British fleet. The latter's prime
duty must now have been intercepting raiding parties before
they could land. It has been suggested that the *numerus
barcariorum* at Lancaster was responsible for defence and not
merely for transport of materials. But so far, apart from the
numerus of Tigris bargemen at South Shields, nothing
comparable is known for the east coast.[13] All these northern
forces will have been under the command of the *dux
Britanniarum* who was presumably normally stationed at
York. The *Notitia Dignitatum* has an up-to-date list for part of
his command, and it is noticeable that it, apart from the
outdated sections referring to Hadrian's Wall and some of
its hinterland, consists of the new-style *equites* and *numeri*,
some named from the forts at which they were stationed.[14]
The reorganization of the defences of the diocese by Count
Theodosius seems to have been effective, since not even the
removal of troops from Britain in A.D.383 by Magnus
Maximus, who had the year before campaigned against
Picts and Scots, led to serious trouble.[15] The Wall was still
held, and so were the Pennine forts. Similarly, Stilicho,
Honorius's general, himself a Vandal, took naval action
against Picts, Scots and Saxons and then removed yet more
troops in 401.[16] At this point it becomes impossible to say
which fortresses and forts were being evacuated, but
between 401–7 the remaining units in Britain were withdrawn to the Continent. In A.D.410 came Honorius's
famous rescript, not intended to signal the abandonment of

Britain by the Empire, but rather to confirm its membership of it, though saying that in future the *civitates* would have to defend themselves.[17]

So far we have been dealing with military affairs. What of the civilian population of Brigantia after A.D.367? Towns in Britain as a whole seem to have been capable of modernizing defences by adding bastions to them in the course of the fourth century, some certainly as late as the 350s or 360s, possibly sometimes as a result of Theodosius's actions.[18] The labour involved was considerable, since old ditches had to be filled and new, broad ones cut in addition to the building of the bastions. At first sight this suggests towns which were still flourishing. However, at some sites the foundations of the new bastions (and the new riverside wall at London) incorporated material from public buildings and cemeteries. This analogy with what happened in Gaul in the 270s could be taken as evidence that town life was no longer centred around public amenities as it had been previously.[19] But, equally, much of the material could be from temples or other monuments regarded as pagan. In conjunction with the evidence for disuse of the *fora* at Wroxeter and Silchester, and of reuse of the baths at Wroxeter for other purposes, we might arrive at a gloomy view of late Romano-British town life.[20] There is, however, evidence of private building continuing to the end of the century in some southern towns. In Brigantia, only Aldborough is akin to the southern towns in having bastions, though it is not possible to suggest a date any more precise than the mid-fourth century.[21] So far as is known, Catterick and Corbridge had no bastions, and it is quite impossible to say whether the *colonia* at York had them or not.

Structurally Aldborough has nothing to offer demonstrably later than the bastions of the town wall except late repairs to the wall, possibly when one of the bastions was in ruins.[22] A breach 2.5 m (*c.* 8 ft) wide near the southeast corner went down to the footings, and at least 15 m (*c.* 49 ft) of the wall was reduced to the lowest two or three courses. The subsequent rebuilding had a face of crude masonry, including blocks from the angle bastion, retaining a mass of mortar and rubble not revetted on the inside. This rebuilding was not dated in the excavations, but the construction trench for it cuts through a layer of unspecified nature two to three feet thick overlying the rampart. Since no enemy in his right mind would occupy himself with tearing down 15 m (c. 49 ft) or more of town wall, it is much more likely that the wall and bastion had been systematically robbed at some date before the crude repairs.[23] The rebuilding is surely likely to be post-Roman, like the repairs to the breach in the fortress wall at York.[24] Aldborough's coin series goes down strongly to Gratian (18 coins of 367–83). Coins definitely minted after 375 amount to 21 including one of Honorius: this is a large collection for a northern site.[25]

At York we have some evidence of extra-mural building in the later fourth century both outside the fortress, where a house in Aldwark had a late fourth-century mosaic of the Petuarian School, and also outside the *colonia* when a substantial fourth-century house at Clementhorpe was later enlarged and given a polygonal apse.[26] Inside the *colonia* the house at Bishophill Senior shows the same pattern as the Clementhorpe one, and has pottery going down to the end of the century, as does the neighbouring site.[27] Another house at Bishophill Junior seems to show the same pattern initially. Built in the late third century it had an apse added to it, subsequently was enlarged; but by the later fourth century it seems to have been turned over, at least partly, to processing fish.[28] Elsewhere in the *colonia*, near the last house, a stone building partly encroached on one of the *colonia* roads; and a nearby building was apparently out of use, since it had a large pit cut through its floor by, or soon after, the middle of the fourth century. This pit contained building debris.[29] Another possible sign of deterioration in standards has been noted at Tanner Row, where pits and a gully containing fourth century pottery had been cut into the main road through the *colonia*.[30] However, these intrusions could be post-Roman, as could some of the late levels in the *colonia* which contain much building debris. On the whole at York, evidence for a flourishing state of affairs seems to predominate.

Corbridge has a coin series going down to the end of the fourth century, including 13 of A.D.383–95 in contrast to

520 or more of 364–83. But these figures need not reflect any less intense occupation of the site.[31] The military enclosure with the metal-working shop still seems to be extant in the period after A.D.367.[32]

It is only at Catterick, however, that we can be sure of new military activity in the late fourth century. There were drastic alterations then to the building in *Insula* VII which John Wacher takes to be due to the provision of quarters and administrative buildings for a military unit that has left spears, javelins, a lance head, and buckles as well as the spurs which suggest a late Roman mounted unit.[33] How the presence of such a unit affected the town as a whole is unknown, but it would be difficult to suppose complete civilian evacuation.

It will be seen from the above brief account that there is little sign of any major breakdown in town life in the late fourth century, even if military elements were present. Possible suspicions of deteriorating standards at York are balanced by undoubtedly flourishing houses at the same town. Unfortunately we cannot speak of administrative buildings which elsewhere in Britain do sometimes appear to have been in decline at this period, or to have been converted to other uses.[34]

Similarly what we know of the Brigantian villas seems to suggest sites going down to the late fourth or early fifth century with intense occupation, if we may judge from the quantities of Crambeck and Huntcliff wares present. However, both at Gargrave and at Beadlam the principal early houses seem to have been abandoned, and probably robbed, during the course of the fourth century.[35] It is, however, impossible to say what this means in terms of the owners, especially as at Gargrave there is a strong suspicion that a new house may have been provided on another part of the site. The final activity attested at Gargrave was the use of a hearth constructed from tiles fallen from the roof of the north house. Significantly this overlay fallen wall-plaster, and it was probably used to cook a meal, or meals, by a shepherd sheltering in the ruins of the building.

Undoubtedly the disappearance of the Roman army and officials early in the fifth century will have thrown both defence and administration entirely onto local communities. Evidently, in some Roman towns further south, a sub-Roman administration continued to function well into the fifth, if not the sixth, century.[36] In Brigantia, we have no evidence for continued administration from either Aldborough or York. And indeed the *civitas* was so large and geographically diverse that general administration from remote centres would inevitably break down swiftly. Nor is there any sign that the Church was strong enough to replace secular authority. Local administration in the vicinity of the eastern towns, large or small, is another matter, though again evidence largely fails us. Catterick does have evidence for timber buildings which can scarcely be earlier than the middle of the fifth century, but their purpose is undetermined.[37] What is clear is that in the hills, and to their west, the removal of Rome's influence simply meant a return to the old Iron Age tradition, which had probably always lingered just below the surface of daily life. Once more the analogy of the materials used in the post-Roman Irish Iron Age might be stressed.[38]

Archaeologically, we are not helped by the breakdown of the cash economy of Roman Britain. Once the army had gone, new currency ceased to arrive in Britain, and it is thought that by A.D.430 or so coins had ceased to be used.[39] Their archaeological value is thus much reduced in the fifth century. Similarly, the generally disturbed times, leading to such incidents as the massacre evident at the Goldsborough signal station,[40] meant a decline in long-range trade which was also affected by the currency problems. The eventual result was a total disappearance of new pottery from the major centres previously supplying the north. A coinless, aceramic society is exceedingly difficult to assess archaeologically. Late Roman and post-Roman floods in the Vale of York must have increased local problems, though York itself may not have been affected as seriously as was once thought. In addition, the silts laid then have obscured matters further by concealing any sites existing in the floor of the Vale.[41] In recent years it has often been considered that early Anglo-Saxon cemeteries outside towns, such as York, and the presence of certain types of allegedly Germanic belt-buckles, pointed to the use of Teutonic mercenaries in the late Roman

period and by sub-Roman communities.[42] This view is now
going out of fashion, as the early date of the Anglo-Saxon pots
is regarded as doubtful and since the belt-buckles are known
to be standard Roman army equipment.[43]

Burials in cists are often held to be characteristic of this
period, but they are singularly uninformative on wider
issues, although both they and later Anglo-Saxon place-
names may point to possible survival of British communities.[44] We are on more certain, though rarely more
informative, ground when we consider the emergence of
post-Roman kingdoms in the north. Elmet embraced much
of west and south Yorkshire, with a north-eastern boundary
in the vicinity of Barwick and Sherburn-in-Elmet, possibly
marked by some of the linear earthworks of the Aberford
series.[45] The northern point of Brigantia and the Carvetian
area were in the kingdom of Rheged, while another British
kingdom may have been centred on the Craven area.[46] One
might have expected Celtic British kingdoms to have made
use of Roman sites in the Pennines and elsewhere. In fact,
careful search in several sites in our area, like Bainbridge,
Bowes and Ilkley, has shown no trace of such use, either
from structures or artifacts. Any pretention to *romanitas* had
probably disappeared entirely by the later fifth century, and
eventually after the battle celebrated by Taliesin at
Catraeth, usually taken to be Catterick, the Anglian
invaders, long present in East Yorkshire, took over in the
north, the whole process being completed by the time of the
battle of Chester *c.* A.D.615.

All that was left were the Roman roads, the major
monuments of Hadrian's Wall, the walls and fountain at
Carlisle, proudly shown by the citizens to Cuthbert in
A.D.685, and the similar monuments at York. There the
breach in the fortress wall was patched with a tower
probably of the Anglian period, showing that the walls were
basically still in commission, although they were then
perhaps a church enclave.[47] Other evidence suggests that
the legionary *principia* stood, still roofed, until long after the
army had gone. It and its predecessors had stood there for
many centuries, witnesses that the Brigantes had never
entirely become Roman. *Regnum nepotibus Venutii?*

Notes and References

References to British journals normally use the abbreviations recommended by the Council for British Archaeology, which are those of the American Standards Association (list 239,5–1963 revised 1966). Other abbreviations used in this volume are:

AA (3)(4)(5)	*Archaeologia Aeliana* (3rd)(4th)(5th) series
BAR	*British Archaeological Reports*
CBA	Council for British Archaeology
CW2	*Cumberland and Westmoreland Archaeological and Antiquarian Society* (New Series)
RCHM	Royal Commission on Historical Monuments (England)
RIB	R.G.Collingwood and R.P.Wright *Roman Inscriptions of Britain* i (Oxford 1965)
YAJ	*Yorkshire Archaeological Journal*
YPS	*Reports of the Yorkshire Philosophical Society*

1. TRIBAL TERRITORY AND THE PRE-ROMAN IRON AGE

1. Juvenal IV, 196; Seneca *Apocolocyntosis* 12 are examples.
2. Rivet and Smith *1979*, 278–9.
3. Holder *1896* vol.1 col.534; Rivet and Smith *1979*, 278–9.
4. Ptolemy I, 7.
5. *RIB* 933 and *JRS* lv (1965), 224.
6. For the name Jackson *1948*, 57; for the location, Frere *1987*, 46, note 8; Ramm *1978*, 22–4.
7. *RIB* 695; Stevens *1934*, 138; Jackson *1948*, 56.
8. Richmond and Crawford *1949*, 30.
9. Thompson *1967*, 101.
10. Wheeler *1954*, 19 note 1.
11. Tacitus *Histories* III, 45.
12. Ramm *1978*, 39.
13. See note 6.
14. Ptolemy II, 3.4; Ramm *1978*, fig.4.
15. Ptolemy II, 3.
16. Rivet and Smith *1979*, 448.
17. Epiacum, Rivet and Smith *1979*, 360; Calacum, Rivet and Smith *1979*, 288.
18. *RIB* 2091, 2066, 1031, 1053.

19.   *RIB* 630 (Adel), 627 (Greetland), 623 (Longwood near Slack, here *Deo Brigans!*), 628 *(Castleford)*.

20.   It was apparently held as a fort into the late second century, a circumstance which hardly fits with placing it among the Corieltauvi.

21.   For Scarborough, Smith *1927*, 179–200; Staple Howe, Brewster *1963*; Grafton and Roomer Common, Waterman *et al. 1954*, 383–97.

22.   Challis and Harding *1975* part ii, figs.74–5, 84–5.

23.   Piggott *1965*, 207.

24.   Conveniently in Stanford *1974*, fig.2.

25.   Mam Tor, Coombs *1970*, 102; Almondbury, Varley *1976*, 125–8.

26.   Philips *1855*, 26–9 pl.5.

27.   Eston Nab, Challis and Harding *1975* pt.1, 112 and Elgee *1930*, 154–6; Boltby Scar, Elgee *1930*, 157.

28.   Challis and Harding *1975* pt.1, 106.

29.   Ramm *1978*, 26.

30.   Wheeler *1954*, 17–23.

31.   Hartley and Fitts *1978*, 93; Turnbull *1984*, 41–9.

32.   Jobey *1962*, 1–34.

33.   Close *1972*, 23–31.

34.   Ledston, *YAJ* xlix (1977), 12 and 23; Dalton Parlours, *YAJ* l (1978), 7; Roxby, Spratt *1982*, 193–7. For the Magnesian Limestone sites in general, see Riley's contributions to *YAJ* xlv (1973), 20; xlix (1977), 19–33; l (1978), 23–4.

35.   Excavation by the former West Yorkshire Metropolitan County Archaeological Unit, information from Mr John D. Hedges F.S.A.

36.   Raistrick *1937*, 166, *1939*, 115. Recent aerial photography continues to reveal new sites, even in such a well-explored area.

37.   Piggott *1958*, 14; Wheeler *1954*, 20.

38.   Piggott *1958*, 13.

39.   Challis and Harding *1975* pt.i, 139.

40.   Challis and Harding *1975* pt.ii, fig.98; Hayes *et al. 1980*, 297–324.

41.   Challis and Harding *1975* pt.i, 155–6.

42.   Applebaum *1972*, 196.

43.   Challis and Harding *1975* pt.i, 137–8. Orthostats were used in some of the walls.

44.   Wheeler *1954*, 57; Hodgson *1968*, 127–38.

45.   Allen *1963*, 37–8. For Corieltauvi rather than Coritani as the tribal name see *Antiq. J. lxiii (1983)*, 353.

46.   Higgs and White *1963*, 289.

47.   Hencken *1942*, 1–76; *1950*, 1–247.

48.   Jobey *1962*, 19–21.

49.   Challis and Harding *1975* pt.i, 16.

50.   Piggott *1950*; MacGregor *1976*.

51.   Spratling *1981*.

2. HISTORY: A.D. 43–367

1. Tacitus *Annals* XII, 40.
2. Tacitus *Annals* XII, 32.
3. Hartley *1971*, 56; Ramm *1978*, 26.
4. Tacitus *Annals* XII, 40.
5. Webster *1981*, 100; Dool 1985, 15–32.
6. Maxwell and Wilson 1987, 9–10. St Joseph *1969* pl.ii. Neronian samian has been found in field-walking at Osmanthorpe.
7. Ramm *1980*, 28–31.
8. Tacitus *Histories* III, 45.
9. Tacitus *Agricola*, 17.
10. Wheeler *1954*, 21 and 26.
11. Turnbull *1984*, 41–9.
12. Frere in Butler *1971*, 17, Hartley *1971*, 57.
13. Hartley *1971*, 57–8.
14. Frere and St Joseph *1983*, 113.
15. Hanson *1987*, 65.
16. Dobson and Mann *1973*, 198.
17. Tacitus *Agricola*, 20.
18. G. Webster *1953*, 26, for two pigs of lead both dated to A.D. 81, and both with BRIG on one side, presumably (METALLVM) BRIG(ANTICVM).
19. Chester-le-Street, which is attested epigraphically (*RIB* 1049); for other examples see *AA4* xxxii (1944), 88, n.19.
20. In Egypt in the fourth century, auxiliaries were collecting the *annona militaris* and the local fort commander Flavius Abinnaeus was acting as local magistrate (Bell *et al.* *1962*, 18–19). Both activities were restricted to a particular area, perhaps that of the fort's *territorium*.
21. Bowman and Thomas *1983*, 110.
22. Richmond and Gillam *1955*, 221, 230–1.
23. De Laet *1949*, 242–5.
24. SHA *Vita Hadriani*, 5.
25. Hartley *1960*, 113; *1966*, 42.
26. Richmond and Wright *1943*, 116; SHA *Vita Hadriani*, 11.
27. SHA *Vita Hadriani*, 11.
28. Breeze and Dobson *1976*; Breeze *1982*, Ch.5; Hanson and Maxwell *1983*, ch.3; Collingwood Bruce *1978*.
29. For Milking Gap, Kilbride-Jones *1938*, 340–41. Gillam *1961*, 63. For plough marks under Wallsend, Rudchester and Haltonchesters, Collingwood Bruce, *1978*, 58 and 79. Similar marks at Carrawburgh have been published in detail in Breeze *1972*, 85–7.
30. Forts evacuated at this time include: in East Yorkshire, Malton, Lease Rigg (and presumably the other unlocated forts connected with it); East of the Pennines, Binchester, Catterick, Ebchester, Newton Kyme, to which there should probably be added the putative forts at Adel, Aldborough and Healam Bridge. In the Pennines, Bain-

bridge, Brough-on-Noe, Castleshaw, Elslack, Greta Bridge and Ilkley.
31. A.R. Birley *1971*, 82.
32. Collingwood Bruce *1978*, 32. It should be noted that the evidence is only preserved in the central section, and uniform treatment needs confirmation.
33. This has yet to be tested by excavation, but it is difficult to believe that the wall curtain near Heddon would have required repair as soon as A.D. 158 (RIB 1389) because of natural causes.
34. Among recent suggestions is one by Peter Salway which should be noted. He is inclined to consider that Antoninus formed a vast imperial estate out of the Brigantian lands as punishment of the *civitas*. Salway *1965*, 184–7; less firmly held in Salway *1981*, 200–1.
35. Askew *1951*, 14.
36. *RIB* 1389.
37. Robertson *1975*, 87–92.
38. *RIB* 1322; see also Bogaers *1983*, 24–7.
39. Brough-on-Noe, *RIB* 283.
40. Lancaster, *J Roman Studs.* xlix (1959), 106–8; Ambleside, *CW*2 lxxvii (1977), 79–180.
41. For the Wall and the hinterland, see *Britannia* iii (1972), 15–55.
42. Cassius Dio 72, 8.1.
43. Bainbridge, see Hartley *1960*, 114; Ilkley, see Hartley *1962*, 32–3.
44. Collingwood Bruce *1978*, 6–7.
45. That Severus himself was inspecting the Wall at Carlisle (Lugu-valium) 'at a time when he had not only proved victorious but had concluded a perpetual peace' (SHA *Vita Severi* 22,4) may perhaps suggest that the northwest section of the Brigantes was still one of doubtful loyalty.
46. RCHM *1962*, 45–7 fig.35. The enclosure contains a building with associated cobbling later than A.D. 200.
47. *RIB* 1009 (Gelt), 1151 (Corbridge), 1234 (Risingham), 1277 (High Rochester), 1462 (Chesters), 1612 (Housesteads), 1909 (Bir-doswald); *J. Roman Studs.* lvii (1967), 205, no.17.
48. Aurelius Victor 20,18; Eutropius 8,19.1; Orosius 7,17; SHA *Vita Severi* 18,2.
49. E. Birley *1967*, 103–7 shows convincingly that a vexillation from the two Germanies recorded at Piercebridge in A.D. 217 is unlikely to be connected with warfare.
50. Collingwood Bruce *1978*, 8.
51. *RIB* 933 (undated) and *J. Roman Studs.* lv (1965), 224 of A.D. 258–68.
52. For a recent, though inconclusive, discussion of the date of the river front see Butler 1971a in Butler *1971*, 97–9; 104–5.
53. Breeze and Dobson *1976*, 220.
54. Frere *1987*, 334.

3. COMMUNICATION AND URBAN SETTLEMENT

1.   Margary *1967*, 431–41 (80a,b).
2.   Richmond *1949*, 15–31.
3.   Richmond *1925*, 88–94.
4.   Dymond *1963*, 139–40.
5.   Collingwood Bruce *1978*, 106–7 (Chesters), 195–6 (Willowford).
6.   Margary *1967*, 415–17 (28b,c); 417 (280).
7.   Margary *1967*, 367–76 (70b,c,d).
8.   Richmond *1949*, Margary *1967*, 387–9 (74).
9.   Grimes *1951*, 293–302.
10.   Webster *1971*, 65–70.
11.   Wacher *1971*, 170.
12.   *RIB* 1030, 1085.
13.   R. Birley *1977*, 44–6.
14.   *RIB* 1599.
15.   Collingwood Bruce *1978*, 66.
16.   Forty-five of the ninety-three recorded milestones are in Brigantia. *RIB* 2243 (Brough); 2274 (Castleford).
17.   For a suggested late date and a more military nature for this unit, *RIB* 601; Shotter *1973*, 206–9. It should, however, be observed that the inscription is stylistically second- or early third-century.
18.   Recent discoveries in Holland and Belgium show how shallow the draughts of many Roman river craft were. See for instance de Weerd and Haalebos *1973*, and de Weerd *1977*. For Tigris bargemen on the Tyne, see *Not. Dig. Occ.* xl, 22.
19.   *It. Ant.* 465.3 (Isurium), 468.3 (Isuram), 476.1 (Isubrigantum). For a discussion of the name Rivet and Smith *1981*, 379–80.
20.   Myres *et al. 1959*, 52–3.
21.   *J. Roman Studs.* lii (1962), 166.
22.   Smith *1852*, pl.iii. The rooms are misrepresented on all previously published plans, which make them appear too narrow in relation to their lengths.
23.   *Britannia* ix (1978), 474.
24.   Wacher *1974*, 399–401 for suggestion of a *mansio*.
25.   Charlesworth *1971*, 159.
26.   Hartley *1983*, 92.
27.   Charlesworth *1971*, fig.20.
28.   Myres *et al. 1959*, 60; Charlesworth *1971*, 160–2.
29.   Smith *1852, passim.*
30.   Smith *1852*, pl.xviii.
31.   Smith *1852*, 44.
32.   *RIB* 710 G(aius) M(. . .) P(. . .); Kajanto *1965*, 273.
33.   Jessop *1849*, 75.
34.   The Bordeaux inscription of A.D. 237, *J. Roman Studs.* xi (1921), 102, provides the *terminus ante quem;* for Severus's death, SHA *Vita Severi* 19,1.
35.   Aurelius Victor, *de Caesaribus* 20.27; the probability of the techni-

cally correct use of *municipium* by Victor is supported by Mann and Jarrett *1967*, 63.

36. RCHM *1962*, 54b.
37. RCHM *1962*, 52a, fig.41.
38. *RIB* 673.
39. RCHM *1962* fig.38.
40. Ramm *1953–4*, 56–64.
41. Ramm *1972*, 237.
42. Wacher *1974*, 161.
43. The analogies of Rome and Roman London come to mind, but it should also be noted that London was given a river wall in the fourth century (Hill *et al. 1980*, 57).
44. RCHM *1962*, 54–7.
45. Ramm *1976a*, 36–7.
46. The *palatium* or *domus palatina* of SHA *Vita Severi* 22,7 is not specifically placed at York and the context indeed suggests that it was more probably in Carlisle.
47. RCHM *1962*, 56 with fig.46 showing further early walls; Richmond *1947*, 77.
48. RCHM *1962*, 53 with fig. 44.
49. RCHM *1962* 55 with fig.45.
50. It may be observed that multiple public baths are not uncommon in provincial towns, such as Paris (with at least three sets), or St Bertrand-de-Comminges (with at least four).
51. RCHM *1962*, 53; *YPS* (1898), x.
52. *RIB* 657.
53. To *RIB* 678 must be added the Bordeaux altar of Lunaris *J. Roman Studs.* xi (1921), 102.
54. *RIB* 658, with RCHM *1962*, 53b–54a.
55. RCHM *1962*, 57a (for the relief, 120).
56. RCHM *1962*, 51a with pl. 21.
57. RCHM *1962*, 58.
58. RCHM *1962* 53b.
59. RCHM *1962*, 53b–54a, pl. 22.
60. Ramm *1976a*, 40.
61. Carver *et al. 1978*, 29–50. The contrast between the dates of the robbing of the range near the terrace and the bath-suite suggests, but does not establish, the sequence suggested here (p. 35). The awkward relationship of the bath-suite to the rest does not inspire belief in their co-existence.
62. Mr Patrick Ottaway kindly let us see the text of his report on the site, written in connexion with Mr L.P. Wenham, the excavator. Andrew (Bone) Jones has discussed the evidence with us, and his opinion is here quoted.
63. RCHM *1962*, 53.
64. *Britannia* viii (1977), 382–3.
65. Decurion, *RIB* 674; decurion's wife or daughter, *RIB* 683; *sevir, RIB* 678 with *RIB* 687; and a centurion's daughter *RIB* 690.

66. Thomas *1981*, 128 with fig. 29; 237–9.
67. Counted by one of us.
68. *YPS* (1876), 7.
69. Wenham *1968*, 147–8.
70. Wenham *1968*, 148–9.
71. Ptolemy ii, 3.10; Rivet and Smith *1979*, 302–4.
72. Wacher *1971*, 170; 172.
73. Wacher *1971*, 167–70.
74. Wacher *1971*, 170.
75. *Britannia* iv (1973), 279–80.
76. *Britannia* iv (1973), 280.
77. Ross 1961, 63–85.
78. Rivet and Smith *1979*, 322–4.
79. Richmond *1943*, 136–49.
80. *AA*3 viii (1912), 164–5.
81. Richmond *1966*, 76 with pl. viii.
81a. Maxwell and Wilson 1987, 45 now give evidence for denser building south of the main east-west road at the eastern side of the town.
82. Salway *1965*, 50–4; *AA*3 iii (1907) 174–7; *AA*3 iv (1908) 216–44.
83. Salway *1965*, fig. 8.
84. Gillam and Daniels *1961*, 37–61.
85. Faull and Moorhouse (Eds.) *1981*, 143–5.
86. Faull and Moorhouse (Eds.) *1981*, 145.
87. Ramm *1976a*, 3.
88. *Britannia* i (1970), 281.
89. Webster *1971*, 65–70.
90. R. Birley *1962*, 117–29.
91. Hartley *1960*, 110–2.
92. Salway *1965*, 77–81 (Chesters); 84–91 (Housesteads).
93. Compare the regulation for the use of the bathhouse in the imperial mining district at Vipasca. The baths were set aside for women from sunrise until noon, at a charge of one *as*, and for men from 1p.m. to 8p.m. at half an *as* (Frank *1957*, vol.3, 169).
94. For *vicomagistri* see *RIB* 899, Salway *1965*, 179–81.

4. RURAL SETTLEMENTS

1. Riley *1980*.
2. Faull and Moorhouse *1981*, 152 with pl. I B.
3. Frere and St Joseph *1983*, 215 with pl. 34, and references there cited.
4. Higham *1986*, and especially fig.5.1.
5. Clack *1982*, pt.ii, 377–402.
6. Riley *1980*, with fig.14; Branigan *1988*.
7. Ramm *1976b*, 3–12.

8. *YAJ* 1 (1978), 23–4.
9. The classic example is the *prata* of Legio IV Macedonica in Spain, *ILS* 2454–5, with boundaries some 10 to 13 miles away from the fortress.
10. A striking reminder of the importance of lard and beer comes from the Vindolanda tablets, especialy Tablet 4, Bowman and Thomas *1983*, 83–93.
11. Hayes *1966*, 687–700, Close *et al. 1975*, 61–8.
12. Rivet *1969*, fig.5.6.
13. Branigan *1980a*, 18–20.
14. Branigan *1980a*, 20.
15. Definite villas: Beadlam (p. 4 for its inclusion in Brigantia); Castle Dykes (North Stainley); Dalton Parlours (Collingham); Drax; Holme House (Manfield); Kirk Sink (Gargrave); Well (which we accept as a villa not a cult-site). Probable villas: Biggin, Harewood (just under one mile south of Wike); Kirkby Wharfe; Middleham; Old Durham; Sutton-under-Whitestone Cliff; Wilstrop Hall. Possible villas: Birstall; Cawood; Gawthorpe, near Bingley; Moat House, near Newton Kyme; Scarcroft near Leeds; Snape near Bedale; Snapethorpe Hall, Wakefield.
16. For Old Durham and Holme House, Clack *1982*, 382 (plans); Higham *1986*, 199–201.
17. Whether such houses had upper floors, possibly confined to the wings, is a debatable matter. That loft-space was used at some houses is suggested by projecting square responds (which look as if they were intended to take timber stairs) at many sites, including Beadlam, Gargrave, and Rudston to name some Yorkshire examples.
18. Wilson *1966*. The occupation was assigned entirely to the third and fourth centuries but only by dating 18 samian sherds to the fourth century, instead of the second or early third century.
19. Gilyard-Beer *1951*, 18–35.
20. Bignor, Frere *1982*; North Leigh, Rivet *1969*, fig.2.4.
21. Stead *1976*, 26ff; 39ff.
22. Atkinson *1928*, 208.
23. Heslington *1867*, with Lukis *1875*, plan 1.
24. *Britannia* x (1979), 288.
25. Stead *1971*, 180–2 with fig.3. Mr A. Pacitto tells us that this is also his opinion.
26. Possible examples may be quoted from Alresford (VCH *Essex* iii, 37–8); Brading (Price *et al. 1881*, plan, room xxxi); Cox Green (Bennett *1962*, fig.2); Chedworth (Goodburn *1972*, 14); Mansfield Woodhouse (Richmond *1969*, fig.2.1,h); and Pitney (Haverfield *1906*, 326–7).
27. For the question of multiple ownership, see Smith *1978*.
28. Rook *1978*, estimates that a small suite of baths would need 23 hectares (56 acres of coppiced woodland) and the labour of one man to keep it supplied with fuel.

29. Reynolds and Langley *1980*, 41–2.
30. *YAJ* lii (1980), 181.
31. Faull and Moorhouse (Eds.) *1981*, 120.
32. Wright *1946*, 383–86; Richmond and Wright *1948*, 107–16.
33. *RIB* 732.
34. Jolliffe *1942; YAJ* xli (1965), 329.

5. INDUSTRY AND THE ECONOMY

1. Nidderdale, Webster *1953*, 26; Derbyshire, TI.CL.TR. *ibid.*, 18; Mendips, Palmer and Ashworth *1957*, 79 fig.5.
2. Tylecote *1962*, 75.
3. Webster *1953*, 18–20.
4. Webster *1953*, 18, no.14.
5. Richmond *1936*, 109 with fig.2, no.1.
6. Collingwood *1931b*, 81–2 no.8 for a flawed casting from Brough; Collingwood *1931c*, for scrap bronze and flawed castings from Stanwix.
7. Webster *1955*.
8. Jones and Grealey *1974*, 147–53.
9. For a modern summary of the site see Thompson *1965*, 67–87, to which should be added K. Hartley and Webster *1973*.
10. Thompson *1965*, fig.19 and 76.
11. May *1904*, 75–8.
12. Cowen and Richmond *1935*.
13. Ramm *1976a*, 38–9 and 68 (noting the Catterick evidence, too).
14. See note 6.
15. Collingwood *1930*.
16. *Antiq. J.* ii (1922), 99–100.
17. Hawkes *1951*, 194 and 196.
18. Richmond *1945*, to be seen in the light of Thomas *1981*, 220–7.
19. Goodall *1972*, for Langton. For a general distribution map Wedlake *1958*, pl.xix.
20. For the Petuarian School, see Smith *1963*, 96–9 and Smith *1969*, 102–7. The Brigantian mosaics as a whole will soon be published by David Neal, who has kindly discussed them with both of us. He believes that the Wolf and Twins floor is a nineteenth-century production.
21. *RIB* pls. xiv and xv. The stones may be by a Palmyrene sculptor rather than a British one (Smith *1959*, 203–10), but the implication is even more interesting.
22. Challis and Harding *1975*, 23.
23. The large stones at Ilkley (Manor House Museum) presumably came from a mill powered by one of the streams flanking the fort, Hartley *1987*, 32.
24. RCHM *1962*, 141–4.
25. Hebditch and Mellor *1973*, 49 with fig.23.

26. Hagen *1937*.
27. RCHM *1962*, pls.38, 39.
28. RCHM *1962*, 114.
29. Thompson *1965*, 79–80.
30. K. Hartley and Richards *1965*, 32; K. Hartley *1975*, 143–4.
31. K. Hartley and Webster *1973*, 89–103.
32. Dickinson and K. Hartley *1971*, 133–42; additional information from Mr Ian Lawton now confirms the existence of kilns.
33. Perrin *1981*, 58–61.
34. RCHM *1962*, 63b with pl.31.
35. Farrar *1973*, 94–5.
36. Jones *1971*, 64–7 gives evidence for a local mortarium-maker Nator, at Aldborough. For the Corbridge die giving the abbreviated name Satu- *AA3*, viii (1912), 195.
37. Leach *1962*, 35–45.
38. McDonnell *1963*, 410–11 with fig.18, nos.8–10.
39. Kay *1962*, 21–42.
40. Thompson *1965*, 77–8.
41. See p. 82. The only precise figure available for any area in the Roman period is the proportion of woodland for Ausonius's 'little inheritance' near Bordeaux (*de Herediolo* III, 1): arable 130 acres, vineyards 70 acres, meadow or pasture 30 acres and woodland 470 acres.
42. Perforated discs of pottery and stone called 'spindle whorls' occur so commonly in army barracks from the first century onwards that they obviously had other purposes, too.
43. Some arrangement akin to the use of road-tankers in the wine trade will have been needed. Cf. Hinz *1970*, Taf.V.
44. RCHM *1962*, pl.38, no.19.
45. See p. 54.
46. Tillott *1961*, 97 for the frequency of medieval fishgarths in the Yorkshire rivers.
47. Callender *1965*, 51; 78–9.
48. See n.21 above.
49. *RIB* 2059.
50. Bogaers *1983*, 21–4.
51. *RIB* 678 with 687.
52. Birley *1966*, 731, but cf. Bogaers *1983*, 20-1.
53. *J. Roman Studs.* xi (1921), 102. Professor Versey upon seeing the stone in 1971 felt confident that it was from a quarry in the Ilkley area. It should also be noted that the correct reading of line 6 is AB EBORACI EVECT, as personal inspection shows.
54. For the *Britanniciani*, Nehalennia, Domburg and the Colijnsplaat, see Kooijmans *et al. 1971*.

6. A.D.367 AND AFTER

1. The peoples named specifically were the Picts, Scots, Attacotti, Franks and Saxons (Ammianus Marcellinus XXVII 8,5), and we are left to presume that they were the peoples involved in the *conspiratio barbarica* of viii 1.
2. Johnson *1980*, 95; Todd *1981*, 233.
3. Frere *1987*, 247f and 346. Johnson *1980*, 95–6 and Casey *1984*, 76 think of earlier dates.
4. Without combing in detail through all the old excavation reports one can only say that the latest account of destruction in A.D. 367 on site xx will not do (Richmond and Gillam *1955*, 248–9). The latest sherds, including the mortarium fig.6, 29 could all be third-century, and probably are. For the tentative suggestion of destruction of part of the defences at Aldborough, see Myres *et al. 1959*, 49. This is discussed on p. 44–5.
5. Frere *1987*, 351, note 40 with an incorrect reference which should read *AA2* vii (1876), 171–6. But the original report gives no clear evidence of destruction or of the date of the latest level.
6. Ammianus Marcellinus XXVIII 3, 8.
7. At Malton burnt layers were confined to the guard chambers of the northeast gate. In one chamber, however, there was a hearth in use at this period (Corder *1930*, 51). At Bainbridge, one wall of the headquarters building shows traces of burning on the plaster, but there was no destruction deposit in the room. However, the building seems to have been in ruins in the late fourth century, when metal workers' sheds were inserted in the cross-hall and forecourt (*J. Roman Studs.* lix (1969), 207–8).
8. *RIB* 1672–3 (Durotriges), 1843–4 (Dumnonii), 1962 (Catuvellauni).
9. Collingwood *1931* and Bellhouse *1953*.
10. Casey *1979*, 75–6 suggesting the work of Magnus Maximus. For the conventional view of founding in A.D. 369 see Craster *1933*, 253.
11. *RIB* 2022.
12. Daniels *1980*, 173–93; *Britannia* ix (1980), 355–7.
13. Shotter *1973*, 206–9.
14. *Not. Diq. Occ.* xl.
15. Casey *1979a*.
16. Frere *1987*, 355ff.
17. Zosimus vi, 10.2.
18. The latest date for bastions comes from Great Casterton where a coin of 354–6 dates the construction of bastion III (Corder *1961*, 28–9). Cf. Frere *1987*, 248. Recently pre-Theodosian dating has been more widely canvassed (e.g., Casey *1984*, 76).
19. For reused material from major structures, cf. Corder *1956* (Great Casterton); Hill *et al. 1980* (the London river wall).
20. Cf. Reece *1981*.
21. Myres *et al. 1959*.
22. Myres *et al. 1959*, 47.

23. Myres *et al. 1959*, 48 with fig.18, pl.1B.
24. Radley *1972*, 54–5.
25. Myres *et al. 1959*, 63–4. Cf. Kent *1951*, 10.
26. *Britannia* vi (1975), 236 (Aldwark), and *Interim* v, no.1, 32–5 (Clementhorpe).
27. Ramm *1976a*; Carver *et al. 1978*, 39.
28. Information from Patrick Ottaway, who kindly showed us the text of his report, and from A.K.C. Jones for the fish.
29. Mr Ottaway also provided information on this.
30. *Britannia* iii (1972), 310.
31. Kent *1951*, 10. The comparable figures for Aldborough are 10 for 383–95 and 77 for 364–83, Myres *et al. 1959*, 63–4.
32. Richmond and Birley *1940*, 101–2.
33. Wacher *1971*, 171–4 and Hildyard *1957*, 243–6.
34. Note 20 above.
35. We are indebted to Mr A.L. Pacitto for information on Beadlam.
36. Frere *1966*, 87–100.
37. Wacher *1971*, 173–4. For general discussion of Catterick in its context, Alcock *1984*, 14–17.
38. See note 47 in chapter 1.
39. Johnson *1980*, 156.
40. Hornsby and Laverick *1933*, 208; 210; 216–19.
41. Radley and Simms *1971*; Ramm *1971*, 181–3 on York. Recent work on the *colonia* has not produced silts at the levels that would be expected if it too suffered. Aerial photography is, however, now beginning to reveal ditched fields in the Vale, some no doubt of Roman date.
42. Frere *1966*, 87–94.
43. Todd *1981*, 245–8 reassesses the evidence, though still inclines to accept early dates for the pottery. We are grateful for Dr Julian Richards's opinion on the pottery.
44. Faull, and Moorehouse *1981*, 145 and 175–6.
45. *ibid.*, 172–4.
46. *ibid.*, 171–2.
47. See note 24.

Bibliography

Alcock, L. (1984), 'Gwyr y Gogledd: An Archaeological Appraisal', *Archaeol. Cambrensis* cxxxii, 1–18.

Allen, D.F. (1963), *The Coins of the Coritani* (London).

Applebaum, S. (1972), 'Roman Britain', in Finberg, H.R.R., (Ed.), *The Agrarian History of England and Wales* (Cambridge), 1–277.

Askew, C. (1950). *Coinage of Roman Britain* (London).

Atkinson, D. (1928), 'The Roman Villa of Gayton Thorpe', *Norfolk Archaeol.* xxiii pt.3, 166–209.

Bell, H.I., Martin, V. and Turner, E.G. (1962), *The Abinnaeus Archive* (Oxford).

Belhouse, R.L. (1935) 'A Roman post at Wreay Hall, near Carlisle', *CW2*, liii, 49–56.

Bennett, C. (1962), 'Cox Green Roman Villa', *Berkshire Archaeol. J.* xl, 62–91.

Birley, A.R. (1971), 'VI Victrix in Britain' in Butler *1971*, 81–96.

Birley, Eric (1966), 'The Roman Inscriptions of York', *YAJ*, xli, 726–34.

Birley Eric (1967), 'Troops from the Two Germanies in Roman Britain', *Epigraphische Studien* iv, 103–7.

Birley, R. (1962), 'Housesteads Vicus, 1961'; *AA4* xl, 117–29.

Birley, R. (1977), Vindolanda: *A Roman post on Hadrian's Wall* (London).

Bogaers, J.E. (1983), 'Foreign Affairs', in Hartley and Wacher *1983*, 24–7.

Bowman, A.K. and Thomas, J.D. (1983), *The Vindolanda Writing Tablets* (Britannia Monograph No.4).

Branigan, K. (Ed.) (1980), *Rome and the Brigantes: the impact of Rome on Northern England* (Sheffield).

Branigan, K. (1980a), 'Villas in the North: Change in the Rural Landscape' in Branigan *1980*, 18–20.

Branigan, K. (1988), 'An ancient landscape revisited' in D. Kennedy (Ed). *Into The Sun* (Sheffield).

Breeze, D.J. (1972), 'Excavation at the Roman Fort of Carrawburgh 1967–69', *AA4* 1, 81–144.

Breeze, D.J. (1982), *The Northern Frontiers of Roman Britain* (London).

Breeze, D.J. and Dobson B. (1976), *Hadrian's Wall* (London). A new, revised, Penguin edition has now appeared (1987).

Brewster, T.C.M. (1963), *The Excavation at Staple Howe* (Winteringham, Malton).

Butler, R.M. (Ed.) (1971), *Soldier and Civilian in Roman Yorkshire* (Leicester).

Butler, R.M. (1971a), 'The Defences of the Fortress of York' in Butler *1971*, 97–106.

Callender, M.H. (1965), *Roman Amphorae* (London).

Carver, M., Donaghey, S. and Sumpter, A.B. (1978), *Riverside Structures and a Well in Skeldergate and Building in Bishophill* Archaeol. of York fasc.4/1.

Casey, P.J. (Ed.) (1979), *The End of Roman Britain*, BAR 71 (Oxford).

Casey, P.J. (1979a), 'Magnus Maximus in Britain: A Reappraisal' in Casey *1979*, 66–79.

Casey, P.J. (1984), 'Caerwent (Venta Silurum): The Excavation of the northwest corner and an analysis of the structural sequence of the defences', *Archaeol. Cambrensis*, cxxxii, 49–77.

Challis A.J. and Harding, E.W. (1975), *Later Prehistory from the Trent to the Tyne*, BAR 20 (Oxford).

Charlesworth, D. (1971), 'The Defences of Isurium Brigantum' in Butler *1971*, 155–64.

Clack, P.A.G. (1982), 'The Northern Frontier: Farmers in the Military Zone' in Miles, D. (Ed.) *The Romano-British Countryside: Studies in Rural Settlement and Economy*. BAR 103 (Oxford), 377–402.

Close, R.S. (1972), 'Excavations of the Iron Age Hut Circles at Percy Rigg, Kildale', *YAJ*, xliv, 23–31.

Close, R.S., Hayes, R.H. and Spratt, D.A. (1975), 'Romano-British Settlement at Crag Bank and Lonsdale, near Kildale, North Riding', *YAJ*, xlvii, 61–68.

Collingwood, R.G. (1930), 'Romano-Celtic art in Northumberland', *Archaeologia* lxxx, 37–58.

Collingwood, R.G. (1931a), 'A Roman Fortlet on Barrock Fell, near Low Hasket', *CW2* xxxi, 111–18.

Collingwood, R.G. (1931b), 'Objects from Brough-under-Stainmore in the Craven Museum, Skipton', *CW2*, xxxi, 81–6.

Collingwood, R.G. (1931c), 'Roman Objects from Stanwix', *CW2*, xxxi, 69–80.

Collingwood, R.G. and Wright, R.P. (1958), *Roman Inscriptions of Britian*, Vol.1, *Inscriptions on Stone* (Oxford).

Collingwood Bruce, J. (1978), *Handbook to the Roman Wall* 13th edn., Ed. and enlarged by C.M. Daniels (Newcastle-upon-Tyne).

Coombs, D. (1970), 'Mam Tor; A Bronze Age Hillfort?' *Current Archaeol.* xxvii, 100–2.

Corder, P. (1930), *The Defences of the Roman Fort at Malton*, Roman Malton and District Rep. No.2 (Malton).

Corder, P. (1961), *The Roman Town and Villa at Great Casterton, Rutland*, Third Rep. for 1954–1958 (Nottingham).

Cowen, J.D. and Richmond, I.A. (1935), 'The Rudge Cup', *AA*4 xii, 310–42.

Craster, H.H.E. (1932), 'The Coin Evidence from the Signal Stations' in Hull *1932*, 220–53.

Daniels, C. (1980), 'Excavations at Wallsend and the fourth-century barracks on Hadrian's Wall' in Hanson and Keppie *1980*, 173–93.

De Laet, S.J. (1949), *Portorium* (Bruge).

Detsicas, A. (Ed.) (1973), *Current Research in Romano-British Coarse Pottery*, CBA Res. Rep. 10 (London).

Dickinson, B.M. and Hartley, K. (1971), 'The evidence of potters' stamps on samian ware and on mortaria for the trading connections of Roman York' in Butler *1971*, 127–42.

Dobson, B. and Mann, J.C. (1973), 'The Roman Army in Britain – Britons in the Roman Army', *Britannia* iv, 191–205.

Dool, Josephine (1985), 'Excavations at Strutt's Park, Derby, 1974' *Derbyshire Archaeol. J.* cv, 15–32.

Dymond, D.P. (1961), 'Roman Bridges on Dere St., County Durham', *Archaeol. J.* cxviii, 136–64.

Elgee, F. (1930), *Early Man in North-East Yorkshire* (Gloucester).

Farrar, R.A.H. (1973), 'The Technique and Sources of Romano-British Black-Burnished Ware' in Detsicas *1973*, 67-104.

Faull, M.C. and Moorhouse, S.A. (Eds.) (1981), *West Yorkshire: An Archaeological Survey to A.D.1500* (Wakefield).

Frank, T. (1957), *An Economic Survey of Rome*, iii (Paterson, New Jersey).

Frere, S.S. (1966), 'The End of the Towns in Roman Britain' in Wacher *1966*, 87–100.

Frere, S.S. (1987), *Britannia: a history of Roman Britain*, 3rd edn (London).

Frere, S.S. (1971), 'Introduction', in Butler *1971*, 15–19.

Frere, S.S. (1982), 'The Bignor Villa', *Britannia* xiii, 135-95.

Frere, S.S. and St Joseph, J.K.S. (1983), *Roman Britain from the Air* (Cambridge).

Gillam, J.P. (1961), 'Roman and Native, A.D.122–197' in Richmond *1961*, 60–89.

Gillam, J.P. and Daniels, C.M. (1961), 'The Roman Mausoleum on Shorden Brae', *AA*4, xxxix, 37–61.

Gilyard Beer, R. (1951), *The Romano-British Baths at Well* (Leeds).

Goodall, I.H. (1972), 'Industrial Evidence from the Villa at Langton, East Yorkshire' *YAJ*, liv, 32–7.

Goodburn, R. (1972), *The Roman Villa, Chedworth* (London).

Grimes, W.F. (Ed.) (1951), *Aspects of Archaeology in Britain and Beyond* (London).

Hagen, W. (1937), 'Kaiserzeitliche, Gagatarbeiten aus dem rheinischen Germanien' *Bonner Jahrbücher* cxlii, 77–144.

Hanson, W.S. (1987), *Agricola and The Conquest of the North* (London).

Hanson, W.S. and Keppie, L.J.F. (1980), Roman Frontier Studies, BAR Intern. Ser. 71 (Oxford).

Hanson, W.S. and Maxwell, G. (1983), *Rome's Northwest Frontier* (Edinburgh).

Hartley, B.R. (1960), 'The Roman fort at Bainbridge: Excavations of 1957–59', *Proc. Leeds Phil. and Lit. Soc.* ix, 107–31.

Hartley, B.R. (1966), 'The Roman fort at Ilkley: Excavation of 1962', *Proc. Leeds Phil. and Lit. Soc.* xii, 23–72.

Hartley, B.R. (1971), 'Roman York and the northern military command to the third century A.D.' in Butler *1971*, 55–69.

Hartley, B.R. (1983), 'The Enclosure of Romano-British Towns in the Second Century A.D.' in Hartley and Wacher *1983*, 84–95.

Hartley, B.R. (1987), *Roman Ilkley* (Ilkley).

Hartley, B.R. and Fitts, R.L. (1978), 'Comments on some Roman material from Stanwick', *Antiq. J.* lvii, 93–4.

Hartley, B.R. and Wacher, John (Eds.) (1983), *Rome and Her Northern Provinces* (Gloucester).

Hartley, K. and Richards, E.E. (1965), 'Spectographic Analysis of some Romano-British Mortaria', *Institute of Archaeol. Bull.* no.5, 25–43.

Hartley, K. (1975), 'Mortarium Stamps' *in* Robertson, Scott and Keppie, 1975, 142–7.

Hartley, K. and Webster, P.V. (1973), 'The Romano-British Pottery Kilns near Wilderspool', *Archaeol. J.* lxxx, 77–103.

Haverfield, F. (1906), *Victoria County History: Somerset* (London).

Hawkes, C. (1951), 'Bronze-workers, Cauldrons, and Bucket-Animals in the Iron Age and Roman Britain' in Grimes *1951*, 172–99.

Hawkes, Sonia C. (1961), 'Soldiers and Settlers in Britain, Fourth to Fifth Century', *Medieval Arch.* v, 1–41.

Hayes, R.H. (1966), 'A Romano-British Site at Pale End, Kildale', *YAJ*, xli, 687–700.

Hayes, R.H., Hemingway J.E. and Spratt, D.A. (1980), 'The

Distribution and Lithology of Beehive querns in North-East Yorkshire', *J. Archaeol. Science* vii, 297–324.

Hebditch, M. and Mellor, J. (1973), 'The Forum and Basilica of Roman Leicester', *Britannia* iv, 1–83.

Hencken, H. (1942), 'Balinderry Crannog', *Proc. Royal Irish Acad.* xlvii, 1–76.

Hencken, H. (1950), 'Lagore Crannog', *Proc. Royal Irish Acad.* liii, 1–247.

Heslington, T. (1867), *Roman Camps near Ripon with an account of excavation of one of them* (Ripon).

Higham, N. (1986), *The Northern Counties to AD 1000* (London).

Higgs, Eric and White, J.P. (1963), 'Autumn Killing', *Antiquity* xxxvii, 282–9.

Hildyard, E.J.W. (1957), 'Cataractonium, Fort and Town' *YAJ*, xxxix, 246–65.

Hill, C., Millet, M. and Blagg, T. (1980), *The Roman Riverside Wall and Monumental Arch in London* (London).

Hinz, H. (Ed.) (1970), *Germania Romana*, III *Römisches Leben auf Germanischem Boden*, Gymnasium Beiheft vii (Heidelberg).

Hodgson, G. (1968), 'A Comparative account of the animal remains from Corstopitum and the Iron Age site of Catcote, near Hartlepool, County Durham' *AA4*, xlvi, 127–62.

Holder, A. (1896), *Alt-Celtischer Sprachschatz* (Leipzig).

Hornsby, W. and Laverick, J.D. (1932), 'The Roman Signal Station at Goldsborough near Whitby', *Archaeol. J.* lxxxix, 203–19.

Hull, M.R. (1932), 'The Pottery from the Roman Signal Stations on the Yorkshire Coast', *Archaeol. J.* lxxxix, 220–53.

Jackson, K. (1948), 'On some Romano-British Place-names', *J. Roman Stud.* xxxviii, 54–8.

Jessop, C.M. (1849), 'Observations respecting Aldborough, the Isurium Brigantum of the Romans', *J. British Archaeol. Assoc.* v, 73–7.

Jobey, G. (1962), 'An Iron Age homestead at West Brandon, Durham', *AA4*, xl, 1–34.

Johnson, S. (1980), *Later Roman Britain* (London).

Jolliffe, N. (1942), 'Dea Brigantia', *Archaeol. J.* xcviii, 62–87.

Jones, G.D.B. and Grealey, S. (1974), *Roman Manchester* (Altringham).

Jones, M.V. (1971), 'Aldborough, West Riding, 1964: Excavation at the South Gate and Bastion and at Extra-mural sites', *YAJ*, xliii, 39–78.

Kajanto, I (1965), *The Latin Cognomina* (Helsinki).

Kay, S.O. (1962), 'The Romano-British Pottery Kilns at

Hazelwood and Holbrook, Derbyshire', *Derbyshire Archaeol. J.* lxxxii, 21–42.

Kent, J.P.C. (1951), 'Coin Evidence and the Excavation of Hadrian's Wall', *CW*2, li, 4–15.

Kilbride-Jones H.E. (1938), 'The Excavations of a Native Settlement at Milking Gap, High Shields, Northumberland', *AA*4, xv, 303–50.

King, A. and Henig, M. (Eds.) (1981), *The Roman West in the Third Century*, BAR Inter. Ser. 109, (Oxford).

Kooijmans, L.P., Stuart, P., Bogaers, J.E. and Trimpe Burger, J.A. (1971), *Deae Nehalenniae* (Middelburg).

Leach, J. (1962), 'The Smith God of Roman Britain', *AA*4, xl, 35–45.

Lukis, W.C. (1875), 'Castle Dykes', *Archaeol.J.* xxxii, 135–54.

MacGregor, M. (1976), *Early Celtic Art in Northern Britain* i and ii (Leicester).

Mann, J.C. and Jarrett, M.G. (1967), 'The Division of Roman Britain', *J. Roman Stud.* lvii, 61–4.

Margary, I.D. (1967), *Roman Roads in Britain* 3rd ed. (London).

May, T. (1904), *Warrington's Roman Remains* (Warrington).

Maxwell, G.S. and Wilson, D.R. (1987), 'Air Reconnaissance in Roman Britain 1977–84', *Britannia* xviii, 1–48.

McDonnell, J.M.C. (1963), *A History of Helmsley, Rievaulx and District* (York).

Miles, D. (Ed.) (1982), *The Romano-British Countryside: Studies in Rural Settlement and Economy*, BAR 103, (Oxford).

Myres, J.N.L., Steer, K.A. and Chitty, Mrs. A.M.H. (1959), 'The Defences of Isurium Brigantum (Aldborough)', *YAJ*, xl, 1077.

Palmer, L.S. and Ashworth, H.W.W. (1957), 'Four Roman Pigs of Lead from the Mendips', *Proc. Somerset Archaeol. and Nat. Hist. Soc.*, ci/cii, 52–88.

Perrin, J.R. (1981), *Roman Pottery from the Colonia: Skeldergate and Bishophill*, The Archaeol. of York xvi, fasc.2 (London).

Philips, J. (1855), *Rivers, Mountains and Sea Coasts of Yorkshire* 2nd ed. (London).

Piggott, S. (1950), 'Swords and Scabbards of the British Iron Age', *Proc. Prehist. Soc.* xvi, 1–28.

Piggott, S. (1958), 'Native Economics and the Roman Occupation of North Britain' in Richmond *1958*, 1–27.

Piggott, S. (1965), *Ancient Europe* (Edinburgh).

Price, J.E. and Hilton Price, F.G.H. (1881), *A Description of the Remains of Roman Buildings at Morton near Brading I.O.W.* (London).

Radley, J. (1972), 'Excavation in the Defences of the City of York', *YAJ*, xliv, 39–64.

Radley, J. and Simms, C. (1971), *Yorkshire Flooding: Some Effects on Man and Nature* (York).

Raistrick, A. (1937), 'Prehistoric Cultivation at Grassington, West Yorkshire', *YAJ*, xxxiii, 166–74.

Raistrick, A. (1939), 'Iron Age Settlements in West Yorkshire', *YAJ*, xxxiv, 115–80.

Ramm, H. (1954), 'Colonia Eboracensium', *Yorkshire Architect. and York Archaeol. Soc. Ann. Rep. and Proc.* 1953–54, 32–64.

Ramm, H. (1971), 'The End of Roman York' in Butler *1971*, 179–99.

Ramm, H. (1972), 'The Growth and Development of the City to the Norman Conquest' in Stacpoole *1972*, 225–51.

Ramm, H. (1976a), 'Excavation in the Church of St. Mary Bishophill Senior, York', *YAJ*, lviii, 36–69.

Ramm, H. (1976b), 'Roman Roads West of Tadcaster', *York Historian*, i, 3–13.

Ramm, H. (1978), *The Parisi* (London).

Ramm, H. (1980), 'Native Settlement East of the Pennines' in Branigan *1980*, 28–40.

Reece, R. (1981), 'The Third Century: Crisis or Change' in King and Henig *1981*, 27–38.

Reynolds, J.P. and Langley, J.K. (1980), 'Romano-British Corn Drying Ovens: an experiment', *Archaeol. J.* cxxxvi, 27–42.

RIB see Collingwood and Wright *1958*.

Richmond, I.A. (1925), *Huddersfield in Roman Times* (Huddersfield).

Richmond, I.A. (1936), 'Roman Leaden Sealings from Brough-under-Stainmore', *CW2*, xxxvi, 104–25.

Richmond, I.A. (1943), 'Roman legionaries at Corbridge: Their Supply Base, Temples and Religious Cults', *AA4* xxi, 127–224.

Richmond, I.A. (1945), 'A Roman Vat of Lead from Ireby, Cumberland', *CW2* xlv, 163–71.

Richmond, I.A. (1946), 'The Four Coloniae of Roman Britain, *Archaeol. J.* ciii, 57–84.

Richmond, I.A. (1949), 'The Roman Road from Ambleside to Ravenglass', *CW2*, xlix, 15–31.

Richmond, I.A. (1951), 'A Roman Arterial Signalling System in the Stainmore Pass' in Grimes *1951*, 293–302.

Richmond, I.A. (Ed.) (1958), *Roman and Native in North Britain* (London).

Richmond, I.A. (1966), 'Industry in Roman Britain' in Wacher, *1966*, 76–86.

Richmond, I.A. (1969), 'The Plans of Roman Villas in Britain' in Rivet, *1969*, 49–70.

Richmond, I.A. and Birley, E. (1940), 'Excavations at Corbridge 1938–9', *AA*4, xvii, 85–115.

Richmond, I.A. and Crawford, O.G.S. (1949), 'The British Section of the Ravenna Cosmography', *Archaeologia* xciii, 1–50.

Richmond, I.A. and Gillam, J.P. (1955), 'Some Excavations at Corbridge 1952–54', *AA*4, xxxiii, 218–52.

Richmond, I.A. and Wright, R.P. (1943), 'Stones from a Hadrianic War Memorial on Tyneside', *AA*4, xxi, 93–120.

Richmond, I.A. and Wright, R.P. (1948), 'Two Roman Shrines to Vinotonus on Scargill Moor near Bowes', *YAJ*, xxxvii, 107–16.

Riley, D.N. (1980), *Early Landscape from the Air* (Sheffield).

Rivet, A.L.F. (Ed.) (1969), *The Roman Villa in Britain* (London).

Rivet, A.L.F. (1969a), 'Social and Economic Aspects' in Rivet, *1969* 173–216.

Rivet, A.L.F. and Smith, C. (1979), *The Place-Names of Roman Britain* (London).

Robertson, Anne S. (1975), *Birrens (Blatobulgium)* (Edinburgh).

Robertson, Anne S., Scott, M. and Keppie, L. (1975), *Bar Hill: A Roman Fort and its Finds*, BAR 16 (Oxford).

Rook, T. (1978), 'The Development and Operation of Roman Hypocausted Baths' *J. Archaeol. Science* v. 269–92.

Ross, Anne (1961), 'The Horned God of the Brigantes', *AA*4 xxxix, 63–85.

Rowell, W.R. (Ed.) (1963), *Victoria County History: Essex* iii (London).

Royal Commission on Historical Monuments (England) (1962), *The City of York: Eburacum*..

Salway, P. (1965), *The Frontier People of Roman Britain* (Cambridge).

Salway, P. (1981), *Roman Britain* (Oxford).

Seeck, O. (Ed.) (1876), *Notitia Dignitatum* (Frankfurt am Main).

Shotter, D.C.A. (1973), '*Numeri Barcariorum:* A note on *RIB* 601', *Britannia* iv, 206–9.

Simpson, K.J. (1976), 'Belt-Buckles and Strap-Ends of the Later Roman Empire: A Preliminary Survey of Several New Groups' *Britannia* vii, 192–223.

Smith, D.J. (1959), 'A Palmyrene Sculptor at South Shields', *AA*4, xxxvii, 203–10.

Smith, D.J. (1963), 'Three Fourth-Century Schools of Mosaic in Roman Britain' in *La Mosaique Greco-Romaine, Colloques Internationaux du Centre National de la Recherche Scientifique* (Paris), 95–115.

Smith, D.J. (1969), 'The Mosaic Pavements' in Rivet, *1969*, 71–126.

Smith, H.E. (1852), *Reliquiae Isurianae: The Remains of the Roman*

Isurium, now Aldborough, near Boroughbridge, Yorkshire (York).

Smith, J.T. (1978), 'Villas as a key to social structure' in Todd *1978*, 149–73.

Smith, R.A. (1927), 'Pre-Roman Remains at Scarborough', *Archaeologia*, lxxvii, 179–200.

Spratling, M. (1981), 'Metalworking at the Stanwick *oppidum:* some new evidence', *YAJ*, liii, 13–16.

Spratt, D.A. (Ed.) (1982), *Prehistoric and Roman Archaeology of North-East Yorkshire*, BAR 104 (Oxford).

St Joseph, J.K.S. (1969), 'Air Reconnaissance in Britain 1965–8', *J. Roman Stud.* lix, 104–28.

Stacpoole, A. (Ed.) (1972), *The Noble City of York* (York).

Stanford, S.C. (1974), *Croft Ambrey* (Hereford).

Stead, I.M. (1971), 'Beadlam Roman Villa: An Interim Report', *YAJ*, xliii, 178–86.

Stead, I.M. (1976), *Excavations at Winterton Roman Villa* (London).

Stevens, C.E. (1934), 'A Roman Inscription from Beltingham', *AA*4, xi, 138–45.

Thomas, C. (1981), *Christianity in Roman Britain to A.D.500* (London).

Thompson, F.H. (1965), *Roman Cheshire* (Chester).

Thompson, R.L. (1967), 'The Evidence of Place-Names', in Beresford, M.W. and Jones G.R.J. (Eds.), *Leeds and its Region* (Leeds), 101.

Tillott, P.M. (Ed.) (1961), *Victoria County History: The City of York* (London).

Todd, M. (Ed.) (1978), *Studies in the Romano-British Villa* (Leicester).

Todd, M. (1981), *Roman Britain (55B.C. to A.D.400)* (Glasgow).

Turnbull, P. (1984), 'Stanwick in the Northern Iron Age', *Durham Archaeol. J.* i, 41–9.

Tylecote, R.F. (1962), *Metallurgy in Archaeology* (London).

Varley, W.J. (1976), 'A Summary of the Excavation at Castlehill, Almondbury', in Harding, D.W., (Ed.), *Hill-Forts: Later Prehistoric Earthworks in Britain and Ireland* (London), 119–31.

Wacher, J.S. (Ed.) (1966), *The Civitas Capitals of Roman Britain* (Leicester).

Wacher, J.S. (1971), 'Yorkshire Towns in the Fourth Century' in Butler *1971*, 167–77.

Wacher, J.S. (1974), *The Towns of Roman Britain* (London).

Waterman, D.M., Kent, B.W.J. and Strickland, H.J. (1954), 'Two Inland sites with Iron Age Pottery in the West Riding of Yorkshire', *YAJ*, xxxviii, 383–97.

Webster, G. (1953), 'The Lead Mining Industry in North Wales in Roman Times', *Flintshire Hist. Soc.* xiii, 3–31.

Webster, G. (1955), 'The Use of Coal in Roman Britain', *Antiq. J.* xxxv, 199–217.

Webster, G. (1981), *Rome Against Caratacus* (London).

Webster, P.V. (1971), 'Melandra Castle Roman Fort: Excavation in the Civil Settlement, 1966–69', *Derbyshire Archaeol. J.* xcl, 49–118.

Wedlake, W.J. (1958), *Excavations at Camerton, Somerset 1926-56* (Bath).

Weerd, M.D. de (1977), 'Römerzeitliche Transportschiffe und Einbaume aus Nigrum Pullum/Zwammerdam' *in Studien zu den Militärgrenzen Roms* II (Vorträge des 10 Int. Limeskongresses), 187–98.

Weerd, M.D. de and Haalebos, J.K. (1973), 'Schepen voor het Opscheppen', *Spiegel Historiael*, viii, 386–97.

Wenham, L.P. (1968), *The Romano-British Cemetery at Trentholme Drive, York*, Ministry of Public Building and Works Archaeol. Reps. No.5 (London).

Wheeler, R.E.M. (1954), *The Stanwick Fortifications*, Res. Rep. Soc. Ant. No. xvii (London).

Wilson, K. (1966), 'A Survey and Excavation within the area of Scurff Hall Farm, Drax, near Selby, Yorks.', *YAJ*, xli, 670-86.

Wright, R.P. (1946), 'A Roman Shrine to Silvanus on Scargill Moor', *YAJ*, xxxvi, 383–6.

Index